The **Mexican** Mama's Kitchen

The **Mexican** Mama's Kitchen

Authentic home-style recipes

Sofía Larrinúa-Craxton

MQP

Special thanks

To Lupia, Agustin and Oliver.

MQ Publications Limited
12 The Ivories, 6–8 Northampton Street
London N1 2HY
Tel: +44 (0) 20 7359 2244
Fax: +44 (0) 20 7359 1616
email: mail@mqpublications.com
www.mqpublications.com

ISBN:
1-84072-816-7

Printed and bound in China

Contents

Introduction

This book is about family cooking. Writing recipes for it gave me the opportunity to relive old memories and rescue recipes that would otherwise have been lost. The first person I turned to for recipe ideas was my mother. It was great fun reminiscing about family events and favourite foods. My father also has a great passion for food and has been instrumental in developing my love for trying new dishes.

My family, like many Mexican families, is very proud of our cooking. A passion for food, both cooking and eating it, is in our blood. On my mother's side, my great-grandmother Aurelia's Spanish and Cuban roots were reflected in her cooking. My grandmother Enriqueta was also an accomplished cook and to this day we still remember her tasty dishes. My grandmother's home-made food was something special. She made lovely soups – her *puchero* was delicious – and her Basque-style salted cod recipe is still cherished by all members of the family. It's a recipe that we still cook every Christmas without fail. Enriqueta spent her life cooking for a large family but she still managed to almost never produce the same dish twice.

Both my mother, Lupita, and Aunt Margarita inherited this great love for food and they developed their own styles of cooking. Growing up in Mexico City, I learned to cook in a similar way to my mother and her sister – by watching them closely. During the last few months that I lived in Mexico before getting married and moving to the United Kingdom, my mother gave me a crash course in Mexican home-style cooking. She feels that a Mexican girl is ready to marry only when she knows how to cook!

On my father's side, my grandmother Martina had Mexican Indian roots. She was married to my grandfather Lorenzo, who had a Basque heritage. She also cooked delicious meals for large numbers of people – they had eleven children! Martina was well known in our family for her *enchiladas mineras* – a signature dish from Guanajuato, from where my father's family originally came. Agustin, my father, is a food lover and I remember how he used to take me to food stalls and markets when I was little and how we would taste all kinds of exciting foods on our visits. My father loves to cook and there are some dishes that he won't allow anyone else to make. His coconut pudding is highly revered by the family, as is his cooking during the Christmas season, and his sticky almond and pine kernel sweets are always popular.

The Mexican Mama's Kitchen is a compilation of recipes that have been passed down through the generations of my family. It is split into chapters to reflect the way a typical Mexican family would eat during the day.

There are two kinds of breakfasts in Mexico: a lighter breakfast that Mexicans would eat during the week, consisting of a plate of fresh fruit, a glass of orange juice, a cup of coffee and a sweet pastry similar to a scone. The weekend brunch is a heavier and more elaborate meal that is eaten slightly later in the morning. It contains all the elements of the weekly breakfast, but the addition of eggs, refried beans and tortilla dishes such as *chilaquiles* makes it an altogether more substantial affair. One of these brunches alone will carry a person through the whole day. It is customary to celebrate a christening or a first communion with a breakfast buffet afterwards.

Comida, or lunch, is the main meal of the day. Everyone in Mexico stops for comida and most families make a huge effort to get together for such a meal. In many ways, everyday life revolves around lunch-time. In Mexican cities, when people cannot go home for lunch, they use what are called *cocinas economicas*, or economical kitchens. These establishments cater to the lunch-time trade and are places where large quantities of soup, rice, main courses and puddings are made. They generally have a room with tables and chairs, where groups of workers can sit and enjoy their lunch during this sociable time, ensuring that home-style cooking plays a part in everyday life. A *comida corrida*, or menu of the day, is served for a fixed price. Typically, all of the elements of a comida that would be served at home are included.

After such a lavish lunch, Mexicans tend not to eat another main meal in the evening – most people will be content with a modest snack, perhaps a cup of coffee and a pastry, or maybe a quesadilla. However, there are many people, like my father, who enjoy eating savoury snacks. *Antojitos* is a lovely word that means 'little cravings', – they are tasty morsels that are eaten at small street eateries. Antojitos are served all day, but it is a treat to eat them during the early evening.

Mexico is perceived as a land of fiestas. There are a number of celebrations that have been inherited from indigenous ancestors and these get mixed with Catholic holy days. Nowadays, Mexicans celebrate special dates in a person's life, like a birthday or a wedding, as well as those dates that have become well known all over the world, such as the Day of the Dead. This particular festival is full of colour, flowers and food, celebrating the day when the souls of our dead loved ones and relatives come back to spend time with us. They taste the food that we make for them, traditionally dishes such as tamales, pumpkin pudding and bread of the dead, and enjoy the drinks we take for them, such as *café de olla*. They supposedly admire the altars that we build in their memories. It is a solemn celebration in which food plays a large part.

Mexican families tend to be large, so it is common to hold gatherings on weekends. My uncle Fernando was a great influence on our family get-togethers. He lived on a beautiful ranch and every weekend he would invite family (an average of thirty to forty people) to visit. It was here that he would treat us to his famous barbecues.

One of the first things he had built on the ranch was a traditional barbecue that is common in certain areas of central Mexico. It is basically a deep hole in the ground that is built up with bricks, like an oven. The idea is to put marinated meat onto the barbecue and slow-cook it overnight. Once cooked, the meat is succulent and melts in the mouth. The meat's juices are reserved to make a stock and this is eaten separately and served with plenty of tortillas.

At the local *tortillería* (a place where they make and sell fresh corn tortillas), my uncle would buy a towering pile of freshly made tortillas. He prepared lovely marinades and made a whole range of salsas. He cooked beans very slowly all morning and seasoned them with chorizo or made refried beans. My uncle produced a variety of grilled meats and it was delightful to stand around the barbecue, picking and choosing food to your heart's content.

I like to share my own recipes and have enjoyed acquiring new ones on my travels through Mexico. I love to cook for my English family and spend my time holding parties, creating menus, cooking, teaching, broadcasting and writing. I hope this compilation of recipes will give an insight into the traditions and cooking of a typical Mexican family.

Chapter one
Desayuno
BREAKFAST

Mexican-style Eggs

Huevos a la Mexicana

This is a very simple but delicious recipe. It's a bit like an omelette and some people say it's especially good for curing hangovers. It's nice just as part of a Saturday brunch. Serve with toast and rocket leaves or chilaquiles and refried beans.

PREPARATION TIME: 15 minutes / **COOKING TIME:** 10 minutes / **SERVES:** 4

**2 tablespoons corn or vegetable oil ◆ 1 medium onion, finely chopped
3 tomatoes, finely chopped ◆ 2 tablespoons fresh coriander, finely chopped
1 serrano or bird's-eye chilli, finely chopped ◆ 5 large eggs, lightly beaten
Salt and pepper**

◆

1 In an omelette pan, heat 1 tablespoon of the oil and add the onion. Sauté for 2–3 minutes. Add the tomatoes, coriander and chilli. Continue to sauté for a further 2–3 minutes.

2 Add the tomato mixture to the lightly beaten and seasoned eggs. Mix well.

3 Add the rest of the oil to the pan and heat again. Place the egg mixture into the pan and

cook for 2–3 minutes, until the base is set. Fold and turn in the same way as an omelette. Some people like to stir the egg mixture so that the eggs are scrambled – either way is good.

4 Serve with a glass of fresh orange juice, hot coffee, toast or Chilaquiles (see pages 16–17) and Refried Beans (see page 87).

Bricklayer-style Eggs
Huevos al Albañil

*Manual workers in Mexico tend to carry their brunches to work with them.
It's traditional for bricklayers to carry lunch pails to the obra, or building site;
inside the pails are beans, bricklayer-style eggs, pickled chillies and tortillas.
When they take a break in the morning, they heat the food up and eat a delicious
brunch. Sometimes the architects are also invited to join the feast
(if the bricklayers like them!).*

PREPARATION TIME: 15 minutes / **COOKING TIME:** 10 minutes / **SERVES:** 4

2 medium ripe tomatoes ◆ 1–2 serrano or bird's-eye chillies
1 clove garlic, peeled ◆ 2 tablespoons corn or vegetable oil ◆ ½ onion, finely sliced
Salt and pepper ◆ 5 large eggs, lightly beaten

◆

1 With a knife, make a small cross at the base of the tomatoes and place them in a saucepan of boiling water for 1 minute. Remove from the water and peel. In a blender, mix the chillies, garlic and tomatoes.

2 In an omelette pan, heat half the oil and sauté the onion for a few minutes, until soft but not burnt. Add the tomato and chilli mixture and sauté for 1 minute. Season with salt and pepper. Add the sauce to the eggs and mix well.

3 Heat the remaining oil and add the egg mixture. Stir the eggs so that they resemble scrambled eggs – not an omelette.

4 Serve with Back Burner Beans (see page 86), plenty of fresh Tortillas (see page 20) and Pickled Jalapeños (see page 108). These eggs are traditionally served inside fresh corn tortillas and eaten like tacos.

Ranch-style Eggs
Huevos Rancheros

This recipe is a favourite of Oliver, my English husband. The combination of the salsa, eggs and tortilla is so delicious.

PREPARATION TIME: 15 minutes / **COOKING TIME:** 10 minutes / **SERVES:** 4

**3 tablespoons corn or vegetable oil ◆ ½ medium onion, finely chopped
2 tomatoes, finely chopped ◆ 1 serrano or bird's-eye chilli, finely chopped
Salt and pepper ◆ 4 soft corn tortillas ◆ 4 large eggs**

◆

1 Heat 1 tablespoon of oil and add the onion. Sauté for 2–3 minutes. Add the chopped tomatoes and chilli and sauté for a furter 2–3 minutes. Season to taste.

2 In an omelette pan, heat the rest of the oil and fry the tortilla lightly – it should not become crisp, just soft and malleable. Drain and reserve in a warm oven. Fry the eggs.

3 Assemble the dish by putting a tortilla on a plate, then top with some of the sauce, a fried egg and a little cheese to garnish.

4 Serve with extra fresh Corn Tortillas (see page 20) and Refried Beans (see page 87) on the side.

Mama says...
You can try serving one egg with tomatillo sauce (see page 19) and one egg with tomato sauce; these are called 'huevos divorciados', which means 'divorced eggs'!

Red Chilaquiles
Chilaquiles Rojos

Many people like to serve these for breakfast with fried eggs or an omelette. Garnish with refried beans for a hearty meal.

PREPARATION TIME: 20 minutes / **COOKING TIME:** 20 minutes / **SERVES:** 4

2 tablespoons vegetable oil ◆ 1 medium onion, sliced ◆ 2 cloves garlic, finely chopped
2 serrano or bird's-eye chillies, finely diced ◆ ½ teaspoon ground coriander seeds
¼ teaspoon ground cumin ◆ 250g passata ◆ 500ml chicken stock or water
Salt and pepper ◆ 200g tortilla chips ◆ 150g soured cream
200g grated cheddar cheese ◆ 1 white onion, to garnish
150g crumbled feta cheese, to garnish ◆ 1 tablespoon fresh chopped coriander, to garnish

◆

1 Preheat the oven to 180°C/350°F/Gas Mark 4. Heat the oil in a saucepan and sauté the onion until soft. Add the garlic and cook for 2–3 minutes. Add the spices, passata and water or stock. Season and cook about 10 minutes for the flavours to develop.

2 Add the tortilla chips and stir carefully so that they don't break. The chips will absorb the liquid of the sauce. Add some more water or stock if necessary.

3 Put the chilaquiles in an ovenproof dish and cover with the soured cream and cheese. Bake in the oven for about 10 minutes, until the cheese is golden brown.

4 Garnish with onion, feta and coriander leaves. Serve warm.

Green Chilaquiles
Chilaquiles Verdes

Chilaquiles are said to be good for curing hangovers. These are made with tomatillo sauce, and the addition of fresh coriander makes them even better.

PREPARATION TIME: 20 minutes / **COOKING TIME:** 30 minutes / **SERVES:** 4

1 tablespoon corn or vegetable oil ◆ ½ medium onion, finely chopped
1 clove garlic, crushed ◆ 500ml canned tomatillo purée
1 serrano or bird's-eye chilli, finely chopped ◆ 1 tablespoon fresh coriander, finely chopped
½ teaspoon salt ◆ ½ teaspoon sugar ◆ ¼ teaspoon bicarbonate of soda ◆ Salt and pepper
225g lightly salted tortilla chips ◆ 500ml water or stock
225g grated cheddar cheese
125ml soured cream ◆ ½ sliced white onion, to garnish

1 Preheat the oven to 180°C/350°F/Gas Mark 4. In a medium saucepan, heat the oil and add the onion. Sauté for 5 minutes, until soft. Add the garlic and sauté for a little longer, taking care not to burn the garlic. Add the tomatillo purée, chilli, coriander, salt, sugar and bicarbonate of soda. Add salt and pepper to taste. Cook for 10 minutes, until the sauce no longer tastes acidic.

2 Add the tortilla chips and stir carefully. Add some water or stock if necessary. Season to taste.

The sauce should be quite watery, as the tortillas will absorb the liquid.

3 Put the Chilaquiles in an ovenproof dish and cover with the cheese and soured cream. Bake in the preheated oven for 10 minutes.

4 Remove from the oven and garnish with the onions before serving.

Eggs in Tomatillo and Coriander Sauce
Huevos con Salsa de Tomates Verdes y Cilantro

This dish can be made as an omelette, as scrambled eggs, or simply as fried eggs with the salsa poured on top. If you go for the latter version, try making them like Ranch-Style Eggs (see page 14); just use tomatillo sauce instead of the traditional tomato one.

PREPARATION TIME: 15 minutes / **COOKING TIME:** 25 minutes / **SERVES:** 4

3 tablespoons corn or vegetable oil ◆ ½ medium onion, finely chopped ◆ 1 clove garlic, finely chopped ◆ 250ml canned tomatillo purée (see 'Mama says' if using fresh)
1 serrano or bird's-eye chilli, finely chopped ◆ 1 tablespoon fresh coriander, finely chopped
½ teaspoon salt ◆ ½ teaspoon sugar ◆ ¼ teaspoon bicarbonate of soda (used to counteract the acidity of tomatillos) ◆ 4–6 large eggs, lightly beaten ◆ Salt and pepper

1 In a medium-sized saucepan, heat 1 tablespoon of the oil and add the onion. Sauté for 5 minutes, until soft. Add the garlic and sauté for a little longer. Add the tomatillo purée, chilli, coriander, salt, sugar and bicarbonate of soda. Cook for 10 minutes, until the sauce is tempered and no longer too acidic when tasted.

2 Add the sauce to the beaten eggs and mix well. Season. Add the rest of the oil to an omelette pan and heat. Place the egg mixture into the pan and cook for a few minutes, until the base is set. Fold and turn in the same way as an omelette. Some people like to stir the egg mixture so that the eggs are scrambled; both are good.

3 Serve with fresh warm Tortillas (see page 20) and Refried Beans (see page 87).

Mama says...
If using fresh tomatillos, boil a little water with 1 teaspoon bicarbonate of soda and ¼ onion. Peel the tomatillos and add to the water for 2–3 minutes, until they turn yellowish and soft; then purée.

Tortillas

Tortillas

Corn is our staple food, and tortillas are our equivalent to bread. It might take a little time to master the technique of making tortillas, but it is definitely worth the effort to make them fresh. You will need a tortilla press, a freezer bag, a comal or griddle and a tortilla warmer for this recipe. I always make a large batch and then freeze them. To reheat, put them in the microwave until they are warm and soft.

PREPARATION TIME: 10 minutes / **COOKING TIME:** 3–4 minutes per tortilla
MAKES: about 20

450g masa harina ◆ 1 teaspoon salt
2 tablespoons vegetable oil ◆ 1 litre warm water

◆

1 Mix the masa harina, salt and vegetable oil. Add enough warm water, while stirring. Knead with hands until a smooth dough is formed. Keep covered and damp.

2 Roll a portion of the dough into a ball that is about 2.5–4cm in diameter. Place inside a freezer bag that has been cut open, and put inside the tortilla press. Squeeze until the dough is flat. If you don't have a press, you can flatten the dough by pressing down on the ball with a small chopping board.

3 Heat the comal or griddle so that when water is sprinkled on to the surface, the drops bounce up like balls.

4 Peel the tortilla from the plastic and carefully place on top of the hot comal or griddle. Cook until the tortilla changes colour, about 2 minutes on each side. Remove from the griddle and leave in a tortilla warmer or cling film to cool down.

5 Serve with a savoury dish from this book.

Mama says...
Don't flip tortillas too early when cooking. Wait until their colour changes or the tortilla puffs up like a bubble – remember, practise makes perfect!

Swiss Enchiladas

Enchiladas Suizas

*These enchiladas are delicious and they are usually the first breakfast that I eat
when we arrive in Mexico – the taste of Swiss Enchiladas lets me know that I'm home!*

PREPARATION TIME: 30 minutes / **COOKING TIME:** 35 minutes / **SERVES:** 4

1 boneless skinless chicken breast ◆ 750ml water ◆ 2 tablespoons onion, chopped
1 teaspoon salt ◆ 1 bay leaf ◆ 3 tablespoons corn or vegetable oil ◆ ½ medium onion, finely
chopped ◆ 1 clove garlic, crushed ◆ 250ml canned tomatillo purée (or fresh tomatillos, if
you prefer) ◆ 1 tablespoon fresh coriander, finely chopped ◆ 1 serrano or bird's-eye chilli,
finely chopped ◆ ½ teaspoon salt ◆ ½ teaspoon sugar ◆ ¼ teaspoon bicarbonate of soda
Salt and pepper ◆ 240ml vegetable oil ◆ 6 soft corn Tortillas (see page 20)
300g soured cream ◆ 100g grated cheddar cheese

◆

1 Preheat the oven to 180°C/350°F/Gas Mark 4.

2 Put the chicken breast in a saucepan and cover
with the water. Add the 2 tablespoons chopped
onion, salt and bay leaf. Bring to the boil and skim
anything that comes to the surface. Boil gently for
20 minutes, until the chicken is cooked. Leave to
cool and shred lightly with your fingers. Reserve.

3 While the chicken is cooking, make the sauce
for the enchiladas. In a medium saucepan, heat
3 tablespoons oil and add ½ chopped onion.
Sauté for 5 minutes, until soft. Add the garlic
and sauté for a little longer, making
sure that the garlic does not burn. Add 190ml

tomatillo purée, most of the coriander, the
chilli, salt, sugar and bicarbonate of soda. Cook
for 10 minutes, until the sauce no longer tastes
too acidic. Add some of the chicken stock to
obtain a fairly liquid sauce. Season to taste with
salt and pepper.

4 Heat the 240ml vegetable oil in a frying pan and
put the tortillas in one at a time. Fry each tortilla
for 15 seconds and place on a plate lined with
kitchen paper. The tortillas should remain soft.

5 Dip each tortilla in the sauce and place on a
medium-sized baking dish. Put a little of the
shredded chicken on each tortilla and fold in half.

Repeat the process with each tortilla. Top with the rest of the tomatillo sauce, the soured cream and the cheese. Bake in the oven for 10 minutes, until the cheese turns golden brown.

6 Garnish with the remaining coriander and serve warm. They taste delicious when served with Refried Beans (see page 87).

Mama says...
In Mexican cooking, 'swiss' refers to any dish that features cream as one of its prominent ingredients. Here, soured cream provides a lower-fat alternative to double cream.

Shells

Conchas

Conchas are always part of the array of sweet pastries at any Mexican table. They have sweet crusts that have been cut into diamond shapes to resemble shells. Try serving them with freshly made coffee or Mexican Hot Chocolate (see page 131).

PREPARATION TIME: 2 hours 40 minutes, plus overnight / **BAKING TIME:** 20 minutes / **MAKES:** 14

15g dried yeast ◆ 80ml warm water ◆ 560g plain flour
½ teaspoon salt ◆ 4 large eggs ◆ 225g brown sugar ◆ 110g butter, melted
140g plain flour ◆ 140g icing sugar ◆ 110g butter, softened
1 teaspoon ground cinnamon ◆ 2 teaspoons cocoa powder

◆

1 Activate the yeast by dissolving it in the warm water.

2 In a mixer bowl, combine the 560g flour, salt, eggs and brown sugar. Add the dissolved yeast mixture. Mix for 1 minute at medium speed. Add the melted butter and continue mixing for 5 minutes at high speed until the dough is formed.

3 Place in a large bowl, cover with cling film and leave in a warm place overnight. The dough will double in size.

4 The next morning, remove the cling film and place the dough on a lightly floured surface. Add more flour if the dough is very sticky. Knead lightly and divide into 14 balls.

5 Place the balls on oiled baking sheets about 8cm apart, as each ball will spread.

6 To make the covers, mix together the 140g flour, icing sugar and softened butter with your fingers until a soft paste forms.

7 Divide the paste in half. Add the cinnamon to one half and mix well until incorporated. Divide into seven balls. Add the cocoa powder to the other half and mix well to incorporate. Divide into seven balls. Flatten out one of the balls with your hand so that it is large enough to cover one of the dough balls. Lay it over a dough ball and cut out a diamond shape on top with a sharp knife to resemble a shell. Repeat the process with all 14 balls and leave to rest for 2 hours.

8 Preheat the oven to 180°C/350°F/Gas Mark 4.

9 Place the baking sheets in the oven for 20 minutes. Remove and leave to cool. When cooked, the conchas should sound hollow when tapped on their undersides.

10 The conchas can be stored in the freezer and used as needed. If using after they have been frozen, preheat the oven to 150°C/300°F/ Gas Mark 2 and place the conchas on a baking sheet. Heat for 10 minutes before serving.

Puff Pastry Sticks
Banderillas

Banderillas are what bullfighters stick into the backs of bulls during a corrida, or bullfight – a bit gruesome. These pastries, however, are not gruesome at all – just the opposite.

PREPARATION TIME: 10 minutes / **BAKING TIME:** 10 minutes / **MAKES:** 18

1kg packet of fresh puff pastry ♦ 45g plain flour
110g sugar ♦ 2 large eggs, beaten

♦

1 Preheat the oven to 180°C/350°F/Gas Mark 4.

2 Chill the pastry before using. To loosen it, beat gently with a rolling pin. On a lightly floured surface, roll out to a rectangle, 45 x 20cm. The pastry should be about ½cm thick. Cut with a knife into eighteen 2.5-cm wide strips. Place these strips on a lightly oiled baking sheet, spaced well apart. Brush with beaten eggs and sprinkle sugar over to cover.

3 Make sure that the oven is very hot before placing the banderillas in, or the pastry will take longer to rise and the sticks may fall on one side. Bake the banderillas in the preheated oven for 15 minutes or until they rise and are crisp and golden in colour. Remove and leave to cool on a wire rack before serving.

Slices

Rebanadas

The recipe for slices is similar to that of Conchas (see page 24), but they are prepared in a different way. They are spread with a mixture of sugar and cream cheese. I have found that spreading them with natural yoghurt is very good, too.

PREPARATION TIME: 2 hours 30 minutes, plus overnight / **BAKING TIME:** 30 minutes / **MAKES:** 14

15g dried yeast ◆ 80ml warm water ◆ 560g plain flour
½ teaspoon salt ◆ 4 large eggs ◆ 225g brown sugar ◆ 110g butter, melted
1 large egg, beaten ◆ natural yoghurt, for serving

1 Activate the yeast by dissolving it in the water.

2 In a mixer bowl, add together the flour, salt, eggs and brown sugar. Add the yeast mixture. Mix for 1 minute at medium speed. Add the melted butter and continue mixing for 5 minutes at high speed.

3 Place the dough in a large bowl, cover with cling film and leave in a warm place overnight. The dough will double in size.

4 The next morning, remove the cling film and place the dough on a lightly floured surface. Add more flour if the dough is very sticky. Mould with your hands so that the dough resembles a log. Place the log on a very large, oiled baking sheet and mark out 14 slices with a sharp knife. Brush all over with the beaten egg. Leave the dough to rest in a warm place for about 2 hours. Meanwhile, preheat the oven to 180°C/350°F/Gas Mark 4. Bake the log for 30 minutes or until golden brown. When done, it should sound hollow when tapped on its underside.

5 Cool on a wire rack, then slice into 14 pieces. These slices can be frozen. If using from frozen, preheat the oven to 150°C/300°F/Gas Mark 2, place the slices on a baking sheet and heat for 10 minutes.

6 Cover each slice with a spoonful of natural yoghurt and serve.

Mexican Biscuits
Bisquets

Bisquets are similar to English scones but are made in a different way and have been traditionally served at Chinese coffee shops or 'cafés de Chinos' in the Chinese district in Mexico City for many years. Chinese immigrants specialized in serving delicious Veracruz coffee in a glass with frothy hot milk and a couple of bisquets. These were cut open, grilled with butter and served with jam. When I was little, it was an exotic treat to go to these coffee shops.

PREPARATION TIME: 2 hours 40 minutes, plus overnight / **BAKING TIME:** 15 minutes / **MAKES:** 22

**15g dried yeast ◆ 80ml warm water ◆ 560g plain flour
1 heaping tablespoon baking powder ◆ ¼ teaspoon salt ◆ 4 large eggs
110g sugar ◆ 110g butter, melted ◆ 1 beaten egg, to glaze**

1 Activate the dried yeast by dissolving it in the warm water.

2 Mix together the flour, baking powder, salt, eggs and sugar with the yeast mixture in the bowl of a mixer for 1 minute at medium speed. Add the melted butter and mix at high speed for 5 minutes until it forms a soft dough.

3 Place in a large bowl, cover with cling film, and leave in a warm place overnight. The dough will double in size.

4 The next morning, remove the cling film and place the dough on a lightly floured surface. Dust with more flour and flatten out with a rolling pin. Fold in three and turn, add more flour if the mixture is too sticky and roll out again. Fold in three once more. Roll out the dough so that it is about 1cm thick. Using a 7-cm biscuit cutter, cut into rounds and place on an oiled baking sheet, spaced well apart. Make a circular cut in the centre of each bisquet, about 2.5cm in diameter.

5 Brush with the beaten egg and put in a warm place for about 2 hours.

6 Preheat the oven to 180°C/350°F/Gas Mark 4. Bake the bisquets for 15 minutes or until golden in colour. When cooked, they will sound hollow when tapped on their undersides. Let cool on a wire rack before serving. If using from frozen, heat the oven to 150°C/300°F/Gas Mark 2, put bisquets on a baking sheet and heat for 10 minutes.

7 Bisquets are best served cut in half, buttered and then placed under a hot grill or on a comal. They will brown deliciously and perfume your house with the smell of butter and fresh bread. Serve with jam and hot coffee.

Bows
Moños

Moños are another kind of pastry, like Banderillas (see page 25), although they are more dense. They are delicious when served with hot milky coffee or Mexican Hot Chocolate (see page 131). Try doing what you were always warned not to do at the table – dip the moños in your coffee or chocolate – but don't let your mother see!

PREPARATION TIME: 10 minutes / **COOKING TIME:** 10 minutes / **MAKES:** 12

**1kg packet fresh puff pastry ♦ 45g plain flour
110g sugar ♦ 2 large eggs, beaten**

1 Preheat the oven to 180°C/350°F/Gas Mark 4.

2 The pastry for this recipe must be cold before you begin. To loosen it, gently beat it with a rolling pin. On a lightly floured surface, roll out the puff pastry into a 45 x 20-cm rectangle. The pastry should be about ½cm thick.

3 Cut into twelve strips with a sharp knife. Take one strip and twist it from the middle to make a bow shape. Repeat with each strip.

4 Place the bows on a lightly oiled baking sheet, spaced well apart. Brush them with the beaten eggs and sprinkle the sugar over to cover.

5 Make sure that the oven is very hot before baking the moños or the pastry will take longer to rise. Bake the moños in the preheated oven for 15 minutes or until they rise and become crisp and golden in colour. Remove and leave to cool on a wire rack before serving.

Chapter two

Comida
LUNCH

Pasta Soup with Celery
Sopa Aguada de Pasta con Apio

When I was little, I only liked this type of soup and my father preferred Fried Pasta Soup (see page 34), so my poor mother always had to make two soups to please us both! Mexican cooks often add cooked, shredded chicken breast or roughly chopped chicken livers to this soup to make it more nourishing. These should be added at the same time as the vegetables and pasta.

PREPARATION TIME: 20 minutes / **COOKING TIME:** 25 minutes / **SERVES:** 4 as a starter

2 tablespoons corn oil ♦ 1 medium onion, quartered ♦ 1 whole clove garlic
80ml passata ♦ 1 teaspoon vegetable bouillon powder ♦ 600ml water
1 teaspoon salt ♦ 1 carrot, diced ♦ 1 stick celery, diced
50g small pasta shapes

♦

1 Heat the oil in a medium-sized saucepan. Add the onion and garlic to the pan and sauté, stirring for about 5 minutes, until the onion is soft.

2 Add the passata, bouillon powder, water and salt and bring to the boil. Once the mixture has reached boiling point, remove from the heat and leave to cool. Pass the mixture through a blender until smooth and then return to the pan.

3 Add the carrot, celery and pasta shapes to the mixture and simmer for 10 minutes, stirring occasionally so that the pasta does not stick to the base of the pan.

4 Check that the pasta is cooked, then remove from the heat and leave to rest for about 2 minutes. If the soup is too thick, add more water.

5 Serve with warm tortillas and add sliced avocado or salsa (optional).

Mama says...
Never bring soup to the boil, as this impairs the flavours.

Aunt Irma's Lentil Soup

Sopa de Lentejas de la Tía Irma

Most Fridays when I was a child, we were invited to Aunt Irma's for lunch. For me, it was a great treat because it meant visiting my favourite cousin, Mimí, with whom I spent endless fun times. On Fridays it was traditional to eat lentil soup, then Green Rice (see page 50), followed by Salpicón Salad (see page 70). Here is a recipe that is very similar to Aunt Irma's soup – it reminds me of my childhood and of happy times spent with my cousins.

PREPARATION TIME: 25 minutes / **COOKING TIME:** 45 minutes / **SERVES:** 4

200g green lentils ◆ 1 litre water ◆ 1 bay leaf ◆ 2 tablespoons chopped onion
1 tablespoon vegetable or corn oil ◆ 1 onion, finely chopped ◆ 2 cloves garlic, finely chopped
80ml passata ◆ 1 teaspoon vegetable bouillon powder ◆ 1 teaspoon salt
Chipotles in Adobo Sauce, to taste (see page 109) ◆ 1 plantain, sliced

1 Put the lentils in a saucepan with the water, bay leaf and 2 tablespoons chopped onion. Simmer for about 25 minutes or until the lentils are soft but still whole. Drain and reserve the liquid and lentils separately.

2 In a saucepan, heat the oil and add the onions. Sauté for 5 minutes or until the onions are soft. Add the garlic and sauté for a further 2 minutes, making sure it does not burn. Add the passata, the reserved cooking liquid from the lentils and 50g cooked lentils. Add the vegetable bouillon powder and the salt. Combine in a blender or use a hand-held blender until the stock is smooth.

3 Add the remaining lentils, taste the soup and add water if necessary. Add the chipotle chillies, a little at a time, to taste. Add half of the plantain.

4 Serve in individual bowls, accompanied by extra chipotles and the remaining plantain.

Mama says...
Lentils absorb flavours and will need to be fairly well seasoned. Taste the soup frequently as it cooks, and add salt if necessary.

Fried Pasta Soup with Beans and Greens

Sopa de Pasta Frita con Frijoles y Acelgas

This was my father's favourite soup. It's a wholesome mix of pasta and beans and can easily be served as a meal in its own right.

PREPARATION TIME: 20 minutes / **COOKING TIME:** 25 minutes / **SERVES:** 4 as a starter

2 tablespoons corn oil ◆ 1 medium onion, quartered ◆ 1 whole clove garlic
80ml passata ◆ 1 teaspoon vegetable bouillon powder ◆ 600ml water
1 teaspoon salt ◆ 4 tablespoons vegetable or corn oil ◆ 50g small pasta shapes (vermicelli
nests are perfect for this type of soup) ◆ 200g cooked pinto or borlotti
beans (canned beans are fine, but they must be rinsed and drained)
30g fresh chopped Swiss chard, kale or spinach

◆

1 Heat the 2 tablespoons oil in a medium-sized saucepan. Add the onion and the garlic to the pan and sauté, stirring, until the onion is soft. Add the passata, bouillon powder, water and salt and bring to the boil. Remove from the heat and let cool. Pass the mixture through the blender until smooth.

2 Return the mixture to the pan and reserve. In a separate frying pan, add the 4 tablespoons oil and heat until it starts smoking.

3 Add the pasta shapes and, making sure that the heat remains low, stir the shapes constantly until they turn golden brown. Be careful, as the pasta tends to burn quite quickly.

4 Once the pasta has browned, remove from the heat and drain off the oil carefully, as it will be very hot and might spatter. Use kitchen paper to soak up any excess oil.

5 Add the pasta to the reserved mixture and bring to a near boil. Cook over medium heat for about 10 minutes, until the pasta is cooked through. Stir occasionally so that the pasta does not stick to the base of the pan.

6 Add the beans and the greens at the end of the cooking process. Remove from the heat and leave to cool slightly before tasting. Adjust the seasoning to taste, and add more water if the soup is too thick.

7 Serve with sliced avocado and crumbled feta cheese, if you desire. This soup is delicious served with Chipotles in Adobo Sauce (see page 109) or Salsa Molcajeteada (see page 110).

Mama says...
This soup is best made one day in advance. It will store in the refrigerator up to three days, so try to make a large batch.

Chicken Soup from Tlalpan
Caldo Tlalpeno

My mother's favourite uncle was Uncle Eduardo. He had a ranch in Tlalpan, a beautiful place near Mexico City. She remembers the natural beauty of the place she visited as a young girl – there was a cathedral, a square, some convents and a few houses. Nowadays Tlalpan is still beautiful, but there is no hint of the countryside that my mother loved. It has been swallowed by the metropolis that is Mexico City. One of my earliest memories is of going to Tlalpan with my parents and eating tacos in the square . . . but that's another story. This chicken soup recipe is typical of Tlalpan.

PREPARATION TIME: 25 minutes / **COOKING TIME:** 40 minutes / **SERVES:** 4

1 large skinless boneless chicken breast ◆ ¼ onion
1 whole clove garlic ◆ 1 bay leaf ◆ 1 teaspoon salt ◆ 4 black peppercorns
1 litre water ◆ 1 carrot, diced ◆ 1 carrot, cut into batons ◆ 1 small courgette, sliced
140g cooked chickpeas (these can be canned, but rinse and drain before using)
½ teaspoon Chipotles in Adobo (see page 109)

1 Put the chicken, onion, garlic, bay leaf, salt, peppercorns, diced carrot and water into a medium-sized saucepan. Bring to the boil, skimming off the film that comes to the surface. Boil gently until the chicken breast is cooked, about 20 minutes. Remove the chicken, leave to cool, then shred with your fingers. Reserve.

2 Pass the stock through a seive into another saucepan and add the chickpeas, carrot batons and courgette to the stock. Cook uncovered over a low heat for 20 minutes or until the vegetables are cooked. Put the shredded chicken back in the stock. Add the chipotles.

3 Serve with more chipotles, lime wedges, chopped fresh coriander and warm fresh Tortillas (see page 20).

Mama says...
Never add all the chipotles at once; add a small amount first and taste.

Fish Soup
Sopa de Pescado

Every Friday during Lent, we were not allowed to eat red meat, so we always ate fish instead. My mother used to make this fish soup recipe, which was handed down from her mother.

PREPARATION TIME: 25 minutes / **COOKING TIME:** 20 minutes / **SERVES:** 6

1 large dried ancho chilli, deseeded ◆ 250ml water ◆ 4 large tomatoes or equivalent canned chopped tomatoes ◆ 4 whole cloves garlic, unpeeled ◆ 1 tablespoon vegetable oil 1 medium onion, sliced ◆ 2 bay leaves ◆ 3 cloves ◆ 5 black peppercorns ½ teaspoon dried oregano ◆ Salt 2 fresh white fish fillets, diced (reserve the heads and tails for the stock)

◆

1 Cut the chilli into large pieces and place in 250ml hot water to steep.

2 Preheat the grill. Cut a small cross at the base of the tomatoes. Roast the tomatoes under the grill until their skins blacken, then remove from the heat and peel. Quarter them and place in a mixer bowl (if using canned tomatoes, put these straight into the bowl). Grill the garlic cloves in their skins until they are soft. Peel and add them to the mixer bowl. Add the chillies. Blend well until the ingredients are puréed.

3 In a large pan, heat the oil and sauté the onion until it is soft. Add the tomato and chilli mixture. Cook for a further 2 minutes, stirring constantly.

4 Add 1 litre water, the bay leaves, cloves, peppercorns and oregano. Add salt to taste. At this stage, if the soup looks too thin, simmer to reduce. Add the diced fish, fish heads and tails. Simmer gently for a further 10 minutes.

5 Remove the heads and tails and serve the soup hot with lime wedges, Salsa Molcajeteada (see page 110) and chopped coriander to garnish.

Mama says...
Add the fish near the end of the cooking time, as it cooks very quickly in the soup.

Mexican Beef Soup

Mole de Olla

Like most things in Mexico, this soup is a marriage between the Spanish soup called
Puchero and Mexican chillies. In this soup, the chillies give flavour, colour and a
little heat. A bowl of Mole de Olla is a meal in itself; serve it in small bowls if it is
to be part of a Mexican comida. Because it benefits from a long cooking time,
it's best made a day in advance.

PREPARATION TIME: 35 minutes / **COOKING TIME:** 1 hour 30 minutes in a normal saucepan,
40 minutes in a pressure cooker / **SERVES:** 4–6

450g beef topside ◆ 2 tablespoons sliced onion ◆ 4 cloves garlic, crushed ◆ 2 bay leaves
1½ litres water ◆ 1 teaspoon salt ◆ 4 black peppercorns ◆ ½ dried ancho chilli
⅓ dried pasilla chilli ◆ 2 medium tomatoes ◆ 2 tablespoons roughly chopped onion
140g canned chickpeas (rinsed and drained before using) ◆ 2 courgettes, cut into 2.5-cm
batons ◆ 2 large carrots, cut into 2.5-cm batons ◆ 1 corn-on-the-cob, cut into 5-cm chunks
(if the corn is too tough to cut, leave whole and cut once it has cooked) ◆ 110g green beans
½ chayote (christophene), cut into wedges (optional)

◆

1 Put the beef, onion, bay leaves, water, salt, peppercorns and 2 garlic cloves in a large saucepan or pressure cooker. Bring to the boil. Cook until the meat is soft and tender. This will take a long time, so a pressure cooker is recommended. When cooked, remove the meat from the stock and reserve each separately.

2 Cut the dried chillies open. Deseed and remove any veins carefully. Wear rubber gloves to protect your skin. Cut the chillies into large pieces using scissors and soak them in a cup of the stock or in hot water.

3 Make a cross-cut at the base of the tomatoes. Preheat a grill, and when it is very hot, roast the tomatoes until their skins are blackened. Leave them to cool slightly then peel. Repeat the process with the other two garlic cloves. Grill in their skin until soft and peel when cool.

4 Blend the chillies, tomatoes, onion and garlic with some of the meat stock. Add the chilli mixture to the reserved stock and strain into a bowl. The strained stock will be clear and dark in colour.

5 Pour the stock into a large saucepan. Remove any fatty pieces of gristle from the meat and discard. Add the meat to the saucepan with the chickpeas and remaining vegetables. Bring to the boil and simmer for 15–20 minutes or until the vegetables are cooked.

6 Serve the Mole de Olla hot in deep individual bowls, making sure that the ingredients are doled out fairly between each serving. If liked, serve with lime wedges, chopped serrano chillies and hot Tortillas (see page 20).

Mama says...
If you have access to an artisan tortilla shop, buy some fresh corn masa (dough), make little dumplings and drop these into the soup. They will cook in about 7 minutes and they make this hearty soup even more wholesome and filling.

Spanish Veal Stew with Vegetables
Caldo de Puchero

My maternal great-grandfather had Spanish roots. He was a very kind man but quite strict, and it was customary at my mother's home to serve Caldo de Puchero every day – my great-grandfather would take it upon himself to serve the broth. It is very rich and takes some time to cook – for extra flavour, it's best to cook the broth a day in advance. This is a more Spanish version of Mole de Olla.

PREPARATION TIME: 35 minutes / **COOKING TIME:** 1 hour 15 minutes in a saucepan, 40 minutes in a pressure cooker / **SERVES:** 4–6

100g bacon ◆ 285g veal bones ◆ ½ medium onion, sliced ◆ 2 bay leaves
2 whole cloves garlic ◆ 450g veal topside ◆ 1½ litres water ◆ 1 teaspoon salt
4 black peppercorns ◆ 200g diced chorizo (use spicy salami as an alternative)
140g canned chickpeas (rinse and drain before using) ◆ 2 courgettes, cut into 2.5-cm batons
2 large carrots, cut into 2.5-cm batons ◆ 1 corn-on-the-cob, cut into 5-cm chunks (if the corn is too tough to cut, leave whole and cut once it has cooked) ◆ 110g green beans
200g shredded white cabbage

◆

1 Put the bacon, veal bones, onion, bay leaves, garlic, veal, water, salt and peppercorns in a large saucepan or in a pressure cooker and bring to the boil. Cook until the meat is soft and tender. This will take a long time in a saucepan, so I recommend using a pressure cooker. When the mixture is cooked, remove the meat from the stock; strain and reserve the stock separately.

2 Fry the chorizo or salami in a frying pan until slightly golden.

3 Mix the chickpea, courgettes, carrots, corn, beans and cabbage with the stock. Remove any fatty pieces of gristle from the reserved meat and discard. Add the meat to the saucepan with the chorizo and cook until tender, about 15 to 20 minutes.

4 Puchero is served in small bowls. Serve very hot with lime wedges, chopped serrano chillies or Pico de Gallo (see page 100) and French bread.

Papa's Shrimp Broth

Caldo de Camaron de Mi Papa

In some Mexican cantinas, you are served a shrimp broth with your drinks, compliments of the chef. My dad acquired this recipe from one of these cantinas and prepared this dish on Saturdays. He used to serve it with a glass of tequila or beer, and with snacks such as guacamole, tacos and chicharron (pork crackling). This soup is a great winter warmer and also very good for helping to cure hangovers. Unlike most soups, this broth is meant to taste medium to spicy-hot.

PREPARATION TIME: 20 minutes / **COOKING TIME:** 30 minutes / **SERVES:** 6

1 litre water ◆ 1 sprig fresh flat-leaf parsley ◆ 1 sprig fresh thyme
1 sprig fresh oregano ◆ 1 large onion, quartered ◆ 1 fish head, rinsed
1 medium-sized fish, back bones only, rinsed
250g dried shrimp (found at Asian markets) ◆ 4 medium floury
potatoes (e.g., King Edward), diced ◆ 4 large carrots, diced ◆ 1 dried pasilla chilli
250ml water ◆ Salt and pepper ◆ 3 limes, cut into wedges

◆

1 Put the water, herbs and three-quarters of the onion into a large saucepan and bring to the boil. Once the mixture starts boiling, add the fish head and the bones. Simmer for 10 minutes. Strain the stock.

2 Put the stock in a saucepan and add the shrimp, potatoes and carrots. Simmer until the vegetables are cooked, about 10 minutes.

3 Meanwhile, deseed the chilli and cut into large pieces. Soak in 250ml hot water, blend with the remaining onion and pass through a seive.

4 Once the vegetables are cooked in the broth, add the chilli mixture. Simmer for a further 10 minutes. Add salt and pepper.

5 Serve hot in individual bowls with lime wedges, if liked.

Aunt Maria's Bean Soup
Sopa de Frijol de la Tía Maria

Aunt Maria was an excellent cook – she always used to make this soup for the children in our family, as she knew it was our favourite. To make it more suitable for adult palates, I've added toasted chillies, crispy tortilla strips and feta cheese.

PREPARATION TIME: 20 minutes / **COOKING TIME:** 1 hour 30 minutes, plus overnight soaking if using dried beans / **SERVES:** 4–6

140g dried pinto or borlotti beans ◆ 2 litres water ◆ ½ medium onion, sliced
2 whole cloves garlic, peeled ◆ 2 bay leaves ◆ 2 large tomatoes ◆ ¼ onion, diced
Salt and pepper ◆ 1 tablespoon corn oil ◆ 3 stale tortillas, cut into strips
1 ancho chilli, deseeded and cut into thin strips ◆ 170g crumbled feta cheese

◆

1 Put the dried beans in a saucepan, cover with water and soak overnight.

2 The next morning, bring them to the boil in the same water and skim off any film that comes to the surface. Add the onion, garlic and bay leaves. Do not add any salt at this stage or the beans will become tough. Cook for about 1 hour or until the beans are tender.

3 When the beans are cooked, put in a mixer bowl and blend to a purée.

4 Preheat the grill. Make a crosscut at the base of each tomato and roast them under the grill until their skins blacken. Peel the tomatoes and blend with the onion. Add this mixture to the bean purée and add salt and pepper to taste. If the soup is very thick at this stage, add extra water.

5 Heat some oil and fry the tortilla strips. Fry gently until they are golden and crisp. Drain and put on kitchen paper.

6 Serve the soup in individual bowls and garnish with fried tortillas, thinly sliced ancho chilli and feta cheese. This soup tastes good served with Pico de Gallo (see page 100) or Salsa Molcajeteada (see page 110).

Tortilla Soup
Sopa de Tortilla

This is the most Mexican of soups. It is one of those soups that benefits from the addition of a variety of garnishes. Adding them is half the fun. I have made this recipe at various cooking workshops as well as for countless dinner parties, and people love it.

PREPARATION TIME: 25 minutes / **COOKING TIME:** 35 minutes / **SERVES:** 6

1 dried ancho chilli, deseeded ◆ 1 tablespoon corn oil ◆ 1 medium onion, finely chopped
2 cloves garlic, finely chopped ◆ 4 tomatoes, chopped
1½ litres chicken or vegetable stock ◆ 30 yellow or white plain corn tortilla chips
Salt and pepper ◆ 4 limes, halved ◆ 2 avocados, peeled, stoned and sliced
110g feta cheese ◆ 110g soured cream ◆ Half bunch fresh coriander, finely chopped

◆

1 Soak the chilli in 125ml boiling water for 5 minutes or until soft. Remove the chilli and chop finely. Reserve the water for your stock.

2 Heat the oil in a saucepan. Add the onion and garlic and sauté for 5 minutes. Add the tomatoes and chilli and cook for 5 minutes more. Put the mixture into a blender. Add 2 tablespoons of stock and blend until smooth. Return to the pan and add the remainder of the stock. Bring to the boil, then turn down the heat and simmer for about 20 minutes. Add the tortilla chips and simmer until they begin to soften. Season to taste.

3 Serve immediately in individual bowls with a wedge of lime to accompany each serving. Garnish with avocado, feta cheese, soured cream, coriander and squeeze over lime juice to taste.

Mexican-style Rice
Arroz a la Mexicana

This is my mother's special recipe. I tried for fourteen years to replicate it in the UK, without success. I blamed the water, the altitude and even the weather. I had to wait for my mother to visit to show me what I was doing wrong. I've borrowed her magic for this recipe and share with you the secret of perfect Mexican-Style Rice.

PREPARATION TIME: 15 minutes / **COOKING TIME:** 25 minutes / **SERVES:** 4

3 tablespoons vegetable oil ◆ 2 whole cloves garlic ◆ 200g long-grain rice, rinsed, drained and as dry as possible ◆ ¼ onion, chopped ◆ 1 carrot, diced
60g frozen peas ◆ 60ml passata ◆ 475ml water
1 tablespoon chicken bouillon powder ◆ 2 jalapeño chillies ◆ Salt

◆

1 Use a deep frying pan with a tight-fitting lid. Add the oil to cover the base of the frying pan and heat. Add 1 clove garlic and leave for 1 minute. Add the rice and heat, stirring constantly for 10 minutes until it turns golden and smells nutty. Add the onion, carrot and peas and cook for a further 2 minutes.

2 Add the tomatoes, water and chicken bouillon powder. Bring to the boil and stir. Add 1 clove garlic and the jalapeños (you can use serrano peppers if you prefer).

3 Add salt to taste. The stock will taste fairly salty at first, but once the rice is cooked, this flavour will mellow.

4 Stir one last time, cover with the lid and reduce the heat to the lowest setting. Leave to simmer for 10 minutes. Do not uncover. Remove from the heat and leave to rest for a further 5 minutes. Remove the lid and fluff the rice with a fork before serving.

White Rice with Feta and Corn
Arroz Blanco

White rice is traditionally served with fish dishes and people also eat it with fried plantains (see page 97). It is eaten more frequently along the Gulf of Mexico, in places like Veracruz and Tabasco.

PREPARATION TIME: 15 minutes / **COOKING TIME:** 15 minutes / **SERVES:** 4–6

2 tablespoons vegetable oil ◆ ½ medium onion, sliced ◆ 2 whole cloves garlic
400g basmati or long-grain rice, rinsed and drained ◆ 500ml milk ◆ 500ml water
140g canned corn, rinsed and drained ◆ 300g feta cheese, crumbled
½ teaspoon salt ◆ 15g butter

◆

1 In a deep frying pan, heat the oil and sauté the onion until it is soft and slightly caramelized. Add the garlic and rice and sauté for a further 2 minutes. Add the milk, water, corn, half of the crumbled feta and salt. Bring to the boil. Give it a last stir, cover with a tight-fitting lid and reduce the heat. Simmer for 10 minutes and then leave to rest for a further 5 minutes.

2 Spread the butter over the rice so that it melts. Fluff with a fork and serve with the rest of the feta cheese crumbled over it.

Spinach and Coconut Rice
Arroz con Espinaca y Coco

*I have to come clean here – this is not a traditional Mexican rice recipe.
However, it is delicious and I often serve it with Mexican food.
All my friends love it, so I thought I'd share it with you.*

PREPARATION TIME: 10 minutes / **COOKING TIME:** 13 minutes / **SERVES:** 8–10

**500g basmati or long-grain rice, rinsed and drained ◆ 175g frozen spinach
125ml canned coconut milk ◆ 1.7 litres water ◆ 1 teaspoon bouillon powder ◆ Salt**

◆

1 Put the rice, spinach, coconut milk, water, bouillon powder and salt in a deep frying pan. Bring to the boil. When the rice mixture is boiling well, give the rice a last stir, then cover with a tight-fitting lid.

2 Reduce the heat to low and simmer, still covered, for about 13 minutes. Remove from the heat and leave to rest for a further 5 minutes without removing the lid.

3 Stir with a buttered fork to fluff and make sure all the rice is coloured green. If you desire, serve garnished with some freshly chopped coriander and toasted coconut flakes.

Mama says...
If this is too much rice for your needs, it is possible to halve the recipe safely.

Green Rice
Arroz Verde

Green rice is delicious and it contains poblano chillies. These can be hot, but when they are cooked in the rice, they lose their piquancy, so you end up with a rice dish with hints of chargrilled pepper flavour and a little spiciness.

PREPARATION TIME: 10 minutes / **COOKING TIME:** 13 minutes / **SERVES:** 8–10

175g fresh poblano chillies ♦ 500g basmati or long-grain rice, rinsed and drained
110g frozen spinach ♦ 1.5 litres water
1 teaspoon vegetable bouillon powder ♦ Salt

1 Roast the chillies by putting them directly into a flame and carefully burn the outsides until their skins are charred. Put them in a plastic bag and wrap the bag in a tea towel. Leave them to steam for 5 minutes. Peel the chillies, discarding the blackened skin (try washing them under the tap). Cut off their tops and remove the seeds. Be careful, as the seeds are hot! Slice the chillies lengthways and place most of them in a blender or food processor, reserving a few for garnish. Add a little water to help the chillies blend more easily.

2 Put the rice, spinach, puréed poblanos, water and vegetable bouillon powder into a deep frying pan. Bring to the boil and when the rice mixture is boiling, give the rice a last stir and cover with a tight-fitting lid. Reduce the heat to low and simmer, covered, for a further 13 minutes.

3 Remove from the heat and leave to rest for a further 5 minutes without removing the lid.

4 Stir with a buttered fork to fluff and to make sure all the rice is coloured green. Serve on a large serving dish and garnish with the remaining slices of roasted chillies.

chapter three

Platos Fuertes
MAIN COURSES

Crispy Chicken Tacos
Tacos de Pollo

Crispy Chicken Tacos are a favourite with the kids. They are extremely versatile. Perfect for picnics, as finger foods at a party or as a simple yet delicious main course or evening snack.

PREPARATION TIME: 25 minutes / **COOKING TIME:** 20 minutes / **SERVES:** 4

2 boneless skinless chicken breasts ◆ 750ml water ◆ 1 bay leaf ◆ ¼ onion, chopped
1 teaspoon salt ◆ 16 soft corn tortillas ◆ 125ml corn or vegetable oil ◆ 16 cocktail sticks
1 head iceberg lettuce, shredded ◆ 300g soured cream ◆ Pico de Gallo (see page 100),
Salsa Molcajeteada (see page 110), Salsa de Tomates Verdes (see page 102) or
Guacamole (see page 104)

1 Put the chicken breast in a small saucepan and cover with the water. Add the bay leaf, onion and salt. Bring to the boil and skim off any film that comes to the surface. Simmer gently for 20 minutes or until the chicken is cooked. Leave to cool and shred lightly with your fingers. Reserve.

2 Take a soft tortilla, put some shredded chicken breast in the centre and spread into a thin sausage shape. Roll the tortilla. The taco should resemble a spring roll. Secure with a cocktail stick.

3 Carefully heat the vegetable oil in a saucepan and drop the taco into it. You can use a deep-fat fryer to cook several tacos at once. Fry until crisp and golden on one side, flip the taco and cook until crisp and golden on the other side.

Remove the tacos and place them on kitchen paper to absorb any excess oil.

4 On a large plate, arrange four tacos, then add the shredded lettuce and soured cream and top with any of the suggested salsas or guacamole.

Mama says...
Be very careful when working with hot oil. Make sure that children are well out of the way and remember that oil spits if it comes into contact with water.

Pimenton Chicken
Pollo con Pimenton

Pimenton is a Spanish ingredient. It is a kind of paprika that the Spanish use as an ingredient for chorizo. Pimenton with tomatoes is very tasty and goes very well with chicken.

PREPARATION TIME: 20 minutes / COOKING TIME: 40 minutes / SERVES: 4

**60g plain flour, seasoned with salt and black pepper (for dusting the chicken)
4 unskinned chicken legs (drumsticks and thighs)** ◆ **3 tablespoons olive oil** ◆ **1 medium onion, sliced** ◆ **2 medium sweet red peppers, sliced** ◆ **1 teaspoon sweet Spanish ground paprika or pimenton** ◆ **Salt and pepper** ◆ **250g passata or 2 large ripe tomatoes, chargrilled, peeled and blended** ◆ **½ teaspoon sugar** ◆ **1 bay leaf** ◆ **150ml chicken stock**

1 Put the seasoned flour on a flat plate. Toss the chicken pieces in it to coat them lightly with the flour. Heat 2 tablespoons oil in a heavy-based frying pan and fry the chicken pieces, one at a time, until crisp and golden. Reserve the chicken pieces.

2 In the same pan, add the remaining oil and sauté the onion until translucent. Add the peppers and cook until soft. You will notice a crust from the chicken and flour in the pan. Stir the crust, making sure that it doesn't burn. Add the ground paprika and season to taste. Add the passata and leave to cook for about 10 minutes.

3 Taste the mixture, and if it is still too acidic, add a little sugar. Add the reserved chicken, bay leaf and chicken stock.

4 Leave to cook for about 30 minutes or until the chicken is fully cooked. If the dish is too watery, you can always reduce it by cooking it uncovered. Test the chicken by inserting a skewer into it. If the juices run clear, the chicken is cooked.

Beef with Almonds and Raisins
Picadillo

Picadillo is a very popular dish throughout Mexico. This recipe has a blend of spices that give it a Middle Eastern twist.

PREPARATION TIME: 20 minutes / **COOKING TIME:** 25 minutes / **SERVES:** 6

1 tablespoon vegetable oil ◆ 1 medium onion, chopped ◆ 2 cloves garlic, finely chopped
1kg fresh beef mince, pork, or lamb ◆ ½ teaspoon ground pimento
3 whole cloves ◆ ½ teaspoon ground cinnamon
500g canned chopped tomatoes ◆ 2 tablespoons raisins
50g Chipotles in Adobo Sauce (see page 109), optional ◆ 1 ripe plantain, sliced
4 medium potatoes, diced and boiled ◆ Salt and pepper
50g toasted flaked almonds, to garnish

◆

1 Heat the oil in a deep frying pan. Add the onion and sauté for about 5 minutes, until soft. Add the garlic and cook for a further 2 minutes. Add the meat and spices, stir to coat the meat and cook for 5 minutes so that the meat has cooked a little.

2 Add the tomatoes, raisins, chipotles, plantain and potatoes and cook until the liquid reduces a little and the tomato no longer tastes acidic. Add salt and pepper to taste. Add a little water if the sauce becomes too dry.

3 Serve garnished with flaked almonds. This dish is best made one day in advance.

Meatballs

Albondigas

Albondigas is a dish of Spanish origin. In my family, we make them stuffed with egg and capers and we give them a Mexican flavour by adding chipotle chillies.

PREPARATION TIME: 30 minutes / **COOKING TIME:** 40 minutes / **SERVES:** 4

500g fresh lean beef or pork mince, or a mixture of both
½ medium onion, finely diced ◆ 2 cloves garlic, finely chopped ◆ 50g stale breadcrumbs
½ bunch fresh flat-leaf parsley, finely chopped ◆ ½ bunch fresh mint, finely chopped
¼ teaspoon ground cumin ◆ ¼ teaspoon ground allspice ◆ 1 egg, lightly beaten
200ml milk ◆ 150g uncooked rice ◆ 2 hard-boiled eggs, peeled and roughly chopped
Capers in brine, rinsed and drained (optional) ◆ 1 tablespoon corn or vegetable oil
1 onion, finely sliced ◆ 1 clove garlic, finely chopped
250g passata or canned chopped tomatoes
2 tablespoons tomato purée ◆ 1 tablespoon Chipotles in Adobo Sauce
(see page 109), optional ◆ 500ml water or stock ◆ 1 bay leaf
Salt and pepper

◆

1 Preheat the oven to 180°C/350°F/Gas Mark 4.

2 Make the meatballs by mixing the meat, onion, garlic, breadcrumbs, parsley, mint, cumin, allspice, egg, milk and uncooked rice in a large bowl until the mixture is fully combined and quite soft. Using your hands, make balls measuring 3–4cm in diameter. Stuff each ball with a little piece of hard-boiled egg and a caper.

3 Make the tomato sauce by making a *soffritto*. Heat the oil in a frying pan and fry the onion until it is soft and translucent. Add the garlic and sauté for a further 2 minutes, making sure the garlic does not burn. Add the passata, tomato purée, and the chipotle chilli. Add the chilli a little at a time and taste frequently until it is as hot as you like. Add the water or stock and cook for 10 minutes. Season to taste. If liked, the *soffritto* can be blended for a richer flavor.

4 Add the meatballs, bay leaf and more stock if required. The sauce should be fairly liquid. Put in a baking dish, cover with foil and bake in the preheated oven for 25 minutes. Season with salt and pepper to taste before serving. This recipe freezes very well.

Mama says...
The meatballs are best made one day in advance for extra flavour. Children will love this dish – try leaving out the chilli if they prefer.

Minced Beef Steaks
Pacholes

Pacholes are thin steaks of beef mince, traditionally made with a metate. They are seasoned with a blend of spices that to me are reminiscent of Moorish cooking – perhaps the Spanish brought this spice mixture with them and the dish got its Mexican flavour from the way it is made. This is one of my father's favourite dishes.

PREPARATION TIME: 15 minutes / **COOKING TIME:** 15 minutes / **MAKES:** 15

**2 whole cloves garlic, roughly chopped ◆ 4 whole allspice berries
4 whole cloves ◆ ¼ teaspoon ground cinnamon ◆ 1 teaspoon coarse salt
3 black peppercorns ◆ ½kg fresh beef mince ◆ ½ medium onion, finely chopped
1 tablespoon fresh flat-leaf parsley, finely chopped ◆ 80ml corn or vegetable oil**

◆

1 Put the garlic, allspice, cloves, cinnamon, salt and black peppercorns in a pestle and mortar (use a *molcajete* – a Mexican pestle and mortar made of lava stone – if you have one). Pound the spices until thoroughly crushed and broken and the garlic has turned into a paste.

2 Add to the beef mince. Add the onion and parsley and, with your hands, mix well until thoroughly incorporated and the meat is soft.

3 Make a ball about 5cm in diameter and put it on the lower half of a sheet of cling film, folding over the top half of the cling film, making sure that the ball is in the centre. Put the ball inside a tortilla press and press until the mixture is very thin. If you don't have a tortilla press, you can

flatten the meat by putting a chopping board on top of the meatball and applying pressure. The steak should be about 5mm thick.

4 In a medium-sized frying pan, heat the oil over medium heat and place the steaks in the oil. Cook for 1 minute, until the edges brown. Turn and cook for a further 1 minute. Remove from the frying pan and place on kitchen paper to absorb any excess oil.

5 Serve with a side salad of sliced tomatoes and watercress, or rocket dressed in a good extra-virgin olive oil. Salsa Molcajeteada (see page 110) is an excellent accompaniment to Pacholes.

Maguie's Beef Ring
Rosca de Carne Maguie

Maguie is the daughter of my godmother Margarita (who is my mother's sister). Both are excellent cooks. Maguie does a lot of entertaining and this recipe is one of her specialities. When I was little, she was my English teacher at primary school and it is partly thanks to her that I was able to understand Oliver, my English husband, when we first met at the Azteca Stadium during the Football World Cup in 1986. Or maybe I wasn't a good pupil after all and Oliver ended up with a Mexican wife when he only wanted to know directions to the nearest cantina! Here is Maguie's recipe.

PREPARATION TIME: 25 minutes / **COOKING TIME:** 30 minutes / **SERVES:** 6

1kg fresh lean beef mince ◆ 100g breadcrumbs ◆ 5 eggs ◆ 250ml milk ◆ 4 poblano chillies, deseeded, deveined and chopped ◆ 100g stoned canned cherries, drained and chopped 125ml grenadine ◆ 250g bacon rashers

◆

1 Preheat the oven to 200°C/400°F/Gas Mark 6.

2 Mix the beef mince with the breadcrumbs, eggs, milk, chillies, cherries and grenadine. Line a ring mould with the bacon rashers to cover the sides. Fill the mould with the meat mixture. Fold over any bits of bacon that are outside the mould and cover with aluminium foil. Put in the preheated oven and bake for 30 minutes. Remove and leave to cool for about 2 minutes, remove from the mould, and serve on a platter, accompanied by a salad of baby spinach and rocket or watercress.

Stuffed Poblano Chillies with Picadillo

Chiles Rellenos de Picadillo

This recipe is a favourite in Mexico. It is one of the most traditional dishes. Poblano chillies can be quite hot or fairly mild. It is always a gamble whether you'll get a hot chilli or a mild one – most Mexicans yearn for a hot chilli! If you don't want to take risks, use green peppers instead. This recipe is labour-intensive and I would recommend making it only for special occasions. Prepare the chillies in advance and, at the last minute, drop them in the sauce.

PREPARATION TIME: 40 minutes, plus the Picadillo preparation time
COOKING TIME: 30 minutes, plus the Picadillo preparation time / **SERVES:** 4

4 poblano peppers or green peppers ◆ One serving of Picadillo (see page 57)
4 large eggs, yolks and whites separated ◆ Flour for dusting
80ml corn or vegetable oil ◆ 2 cloves garlic, roughly chopped
1 teaspoon coarse salt ◆ 3 whole cloves ◆ 4 whole allspice berries ◆ 4 black peppercorns
1 medium onion, finely sliced ◆ 1 tablespoon corn or vegetable oil
¼ teaspoon ground cinnamon ◆ 250ml chopped canned tomatoes or passata
1 bay leaf ◆ 500ml vegetable stock

◆

1 Begin by grilling the chillies. If possible, put them directly into the flame, turning the chillies with a long fork or tongs. The skin should be completely blackened. Put them in a plastic bag, wrap the bag with cling film, and let steam for 5 minutes. Peel with your fingers or a blunt knife, or put them under running water to ease peeling.

2 Make an incision lengthways (see 'Mama says'), and with a small knife remove the part that contains the seeds. Wear rubber gloves and take care, as chillies can be hot and irritate the skin. Stuff the chillies with some Picadillo, or a little cheese if you want to make the dish vegetarian. Close up the chillies and fasten with cocktail sticks.

3 With an electric beater, whisk the egg whites until stiff peaks form. Add 2 egg yolks and continue to beat. Put the flour on a large plate and lightly coat the chillies in the flour.

4 Heat the oil in a frying pan.

5 Dip the chillies in the egg batter. Put them in the hot oil and fry, turning until the egg is cooked and golden. Put the chillies on kitchen paper to absorb excess oil.

6 To make the sauce, pound the garlic, salt, cloves, allspice and black pepper in a pestle and mortar (use a *molcajete* – a Mexican pestle and mortar made of lava stone – if you have one).

7 Sauté the onion in 1 tablespoon oil until soft and translucent. Add the garlic and spice paste and ground cinnamon and continue sautéing for 1 minute. Add the tomatoes, bay leaf and stock. Cook for 10 minutes. Season to taste.

8 Put the chillies in the sauce and simmer for 5 minutes before serving.

9 In Mexico, these chillies are served with a ladleful of sauce. Also, try serving them with Mexican-style Rice (see page 46), fresh Tortillas (see page 20) and some salsa or Chipotles in Adobo Sauce (see page 109).

Mama says...
When preparing chillies, it's easiest to remove the tops and the part with the seeds first. Use the top of the chilli as a lid afterwards if you don't have any cocktail sticks on hand.

Corn Pie

Tamal de Cazuela

My maternal grandmother used to make this for our large family.

PREPARATION TIME: 20 minutes / **COOKING TIME:** 25 minutes / **SERVES:** 6

2 tablespoons vegetable or corn oil ◆ 1 onion, finely chopped
1 teaspoon garlic, finely chopped ◆ 3 peppers, sliced ◆ 3 courgettes, diced
500g Mole (see page 136) or the same amount of mole sauce from a jar, prepared with
water or stock according to instructions ◆ 80g feta cheese ◆ 1 poached chicken breast,
shredded (optional, see Caldo Tlalpeno recipe on page 36 for instructions on how to
poach a chicken) ◆ 1kg canned corn, drained ◆ 1½ teaspoons baking powder
110g butter ◆ 45g plain flour (optional) ◆ Salt and pepper

◆

1 Preheat the oven to 180°C/350°F/Gas Mark 4.

2 In a pan, heat the oil and sauté the onion for about 5 minutes or until soft. Add the garlic and cook for a further 2 minutes. Add the peppers, courgettes and the mole sauce and cook until the vegetables are soft. Stir in the feta. If you want, you can add the shredded chicken at this stage.

3 Put the drained corn in a food processor and, with a sharp blade, blend until it is slightly lumpy and not completely puréed. Add the baking powder and butter and mix well. If the mixture is too thin, add a little flour.

4 Put half of the corn mixture into a greased baking dish. Add the mixture of mole, vegetables and feta cheese. Cover with the remaining corn mixture and season.

5 Put the pie in the preheated oven and bake for about 45 minutes or until a cocktail stick inserted into the centre of the dish comes out clean.

6 Serve on a bed of fresh spinach or with sautéed Swiss chard or kale.

Beef Tempura with Middle Eastern Sauce

Tortitas de Carne Deshebrada en Salsa de Jitomate

Again, this sauce is reminiscent of Moorish or Middle Eastern cooking. It was a favourite at my mother's family table and my grandmother excelled at cooking it. My mother cooks these for me each time I visit her.

PREPARATION TIME: 30 minutes / COOKING TIME: 1 hour 20 minutes / SERVES: 4

500g boneless beef brisket or any cut of meat that can be shredded when cooked, like skirt or flank ◆ ¼ onion, chopped ◆ 1 bay leaf ◆ 1 teaspoon salt ◆ 1 litre water
2 cloves garlic, roughly chopped ◆ 1 teaspoon coarse salt ◆ 3 whole cloves
4 whole allspice berries ◆ 4 black peppercorns ◆ 1 tablespoon corn or vegetable oil
1 medium onion, finely sliced ◆ ¼ teaspoon ground cinnamon
250ml chopped canned tomatoes or passata ◆ 1 bay leaf ◆ 500ml vegetable stock
Salt and pepper ◆ 3 large eggs, separated ◆ 80ml corn or vegetable oil

◆

1 Put the meat, onion, bay leaf, salt and water into a large saucepan. Bring to the boil. Skim off any film that comes to the surface. Cover the saucepan and cook for 1 hour or until the meat is soft. Use a pressure cooker if possible.

2 Pound the garlic, salt, cloves, allspice and black pepper in a pestle and mortar (use a *molcajete* – a Mexican pestle and mortar made of lava stone – if you have one).

3 While the meat is cooking, heat the oil in a separate frying pan. Sauté the onion in the oil until soft and translucent. Add the spice paste and ground cinnamon and continue sautéing for about 1 minute. Add the tomatoes, bay leaf and stock. Cook for a further 10 minutes. Season to taste with salt and pepper.

4 Once the meat is tender, remove from the stock and leave to cool. Cut into 3cm chunks and shred with your fingers. Reserve.

5 With an electric beater, beat the egg whites until stiff peaks form. Add 2 egg yolks and continue to beat.

6 Heat the oil in a frying pan.

7 Dip a tablespoon of the meat in the egg batter to coat it. Put this in the hot oil and fry until the egg is cooked and golden. Turn and cook until the patty is golden all over. Put the tempura on kitchen paper to absorb excess oil.

8 Put the tempura in the sauce and cook for a further 2 minutes. If the sauce is too thick, thin with meat stock.

9 Serve in shallow bowls with a spoonful of sauce, boiled potatoes and green beans.

Mama says...
This dish can be made one day in advance to allow the flavours of the sauce to develop.

Beef Rolls Stuffed with Bacon and Vegetables

Bisteces Rellenos de Tocino y Verduras

This is another dish that is loved by children. In Mexico they are called pajaritos, *which translates as 'little birds'. Just thinking of this recipe, I can recall the smell, the texture and the flavour of these home-cooked rolls.*

PREPARATION TIME: 20 minutes / **COOKING TIME:** 30 minutes / **SERVES:** 6

2 medium carrots, diced small ◆ 2 medium potatoes, diced small
150g frozen peas ◆ 1kg lean beef steaks, pounded thin (ask the butcher
to do this for you) ◆ 5 rashers bacon, cooked crisp and finely chopped
2 tablespoons vegetable oil ◆ 2 cloves garlic, roughly chopped
¼ teaspoon cumin seeds ◆ 3 whole cloves ◆ 1 teaspoon coarse salt
1 medium onion, finely sliced ◆ 250ml passata ◆ 500ml beef stock
2 bay leaves ◆ Salt and freshly ground black pepper
2 tablespoons fresh coriander, finely chopped

◆

1 Boil the carrots, potatoes and peas in water for 3 minutes. Drain.

2 Lay out the beef steaks on a chopping board and top with some of the vegetable mixture and bacon. Roll up and tie with string.

3 Heat the oil in a frying pan. Brown the steak rolls in heated oil, remove and reserve.

4 Pound the garlic, cumin and cloves with the salt until a paste is formed in a pestle and mortar (use a *molcajete* – a Mexican pestle and mortar made of lava stone – if you have one).

5 Fry the onion in the pan in which the steak rolls were browned. Add more oil if necessary and cook until translucent. Add the garlic and spice paste and continue sautéing for a further minute. Add the passata, beef stock and bay leaves. Cook for a further 10 minutes. Taste and adjust seasoning.

6 Put the steak rolls in the pan with the sauce, cover with the lid and cook for 10 minutes or until the meat is cooked and tender.

7 Season with salt and pepper to taste. Garnish with coriander and serve with White Rice (see page 48) or Green Rice (see page 50).

Mama says...
If your butcher won't pound the steaks for you, you can do it yourself by placing them between sheets of greaseproof paper and pounding them with a wooden mallet. They should be soft and about 5mm thick.

Aunt Irma's Beef Salad
Salpicón

*Salpicón is not exclusive to Aunt Irma, and is served in many Mexican homes.
I remember going to lunch at her house and she would serve a very nice Salpicón.
It's a lovely dish for eating outside on a hot day, and is ideal for buffet parties.*

PREPARATION TIME: 30 minutes / **COOKING TIME:** 1 hour 20 minutes if using a normal saucepan,
40 minutes if using a pressure cooker / **SERVES:** 6

500g boneless lean beef brisket or any cut of meat that can be shredded when cooked, like
skirt or flank ◆ ¼ onion, chopped ◆ 1 bay leaf ◆ 1 teaspoon salt
1 litre water ◆ 2 tablespoons olive oil ◆ 1 tablespoon cider vinegar
1 teaspoon Dijon mustard ◆ 1 clove garlic, crushed ◆ Salt and pepper
1 large red onion, finely sliced, or 2 spring onions , finely sliced ◆ 1 head iceberg lettuce,
shredded ◆ 2 avocados, sliced ◆ 500g ripe tomatoes, sliced
Half bunch fresh coriander, chopped ◆ 100g cooked green beans ◆ 50g cooked peas
2 potatoes, cooked diced ◆ 2 bird's-eye chillies, finely chopped

◆

1 Put the meat, chopped onion, bay leaf, salt and water in a large saucepan and bring to the boil. Skim off any film that comes to the surface, cover the saucepan and cook for 1 hour or until the meat is tender. Use a pressure cooker if possible to cut the cooking time by half.

2 Meanwhile, make the marinade. In a medium-sized bowl, mix together the oil, vinegar, mustard, garlic and salt and pepper.

3 Once the meat is tender, remove from the stock. leave to cool. Cut into 2.5cm chunks and shred with your fingers. Coat in the marinade. Reserve.

4 Soak the red onion in cold water for 5 minutes and drain. On a large platter, make a bed of lettuce. In a large bowl, toss the red onion, avocado, tomatoes, most of the coriander, green beans, peas, potatoes and chillies with your hands. Mix with the reserved marinated meat and place the mixture on top of the lettuce. Taste and adjust the seasoning and serve.

Meat with Chorizo and Tomatillos
Tinga

*This dish is very good served as a main course or as part of a taquiza, or taco party.
Tinga, like Picadillo (see page 57), Albondigas (see page 58) and
Carne al Pastor (see page 124) is an ideal buffet food. Plenty of freshly
made tortillas, lots of hot salsa and cold beer are a must,
as is the company of your friends and relatives.*

PREPARATION TIME: 30 minutes / **COOKING TIME:** 1 hour 20 minutes in a normal saucepan,
40 minutes if using a pressure cooker, plus 20 minutes for the rest of the dish / **SERVES:** 8

**250g boneless lean pork, cut into chunks ◆ 500g beef flank steak, cut into chunks
2 cloves garlic, finely chopped ◆ 2 bay leaves ◆ Salt ◆ 500g chorizo
1 onion, roughly chopped ◆ 250g passata ◆ 250g chopped canned tomatoes
5 potatoes, boiled and cut into chunks ◆ 250g fresh tomatillos, cooked and puréed
(see page 102), or canned tomatillos ◆ ½ teaspoon dried oregano ◆ 1 small sprig
fresh thyme ◆ Salt and pepper ◆ 1 tablespoon Chipotles in Adobo Sauce (see page 109)**

1 Put the meat in a saucepan full of water. Add 1 clove garlic, bay leaves and salt. Bring to the boil. Cook until the meat is tender. Leave to cool. Shred with your hands, set aside and reserve the stock.

2 Remove the casing from the chorizo and cut into large chunks. Place in a heavy-based frying pan and fry over a medium heat until lightly browned. Remove the chorizo and reserve. Add the onion and the remaining garlic to the same pan and sauté for 2 minutes. Add the passata, tomatoes, potatoes, tomatillos, oregano, thyme, salt and pepper. Simmer over a low heat for

5 minutes, stirring occasionally. Add the chipotles one at a time, stirring constantly. Be sure to taste the sauce frequently, as the chipotles should enhance the flavour and piquancy rather than make the sauce too hot.

3 Add the reserved meat to the frying pan, stir well, and add 225ml of stock. Add the chorizo, cover and cook over a low heat for 15 minutes. If the sauce is too thick, thin with more stock.

4 Serve in a large dish accompanied by warm tortillas, so that guests can help themselves.

Lamb in Adobo

Cordero en Adobo

This dish can also be made with pork. If you want, try using pork belly or spare ribs. This recipe benefits from slow cooking, like a casserole. Place in a warm oven and cook for a long time.

PREPARATION TIME: 15 minutes, plus overnight marinating / **COOKING TIME:** 2 hours / **SERVES:** 6

250ml orange juice ◆ 1 pasilla chilli, deseeded with top removed ◆ 1 guajillo chilli, deseeded with top removed ◆ 2 cloves garlic, roughly chopped ◆ 2 cloves ◆ 3 black peppercorns ◆ 1 teaspoon coarse salt ◆ 3 whole allspice berries ◆ ¼ teaspoon ground cumin ◆ ¼ teaspoon ground cinnamon ◆ ½ medium onion, roughly chopped ◆ ½ teaspoon dried oregano ◆ 2 bay leaves ◆ 1 tablespoon cider vinegar ◆ 4 lamb shanks ◆ 500ml lamb stock

1 Heat the orange juice and add the dried chillies. Leave to soak. Meanwhile, pound the garlic, cloves, peppercorns, salt and allspice until it looks like a paste in a pestle and mortar (use a *molcajete* – a Mexican pestle and mortar made of lava stone – if you have one).

2 Put the soaked chillies, reserved orange juice, garlic and spice paste, cumin, cinnamon and onion in a food processor bowl. Blend until the mixture turns into a bright red paste. Add the oregano, bay leaves and cider vinegar. Prick the meat with a fork to allow it to marinate better. Place in a non-metallic bowl and add the chilli mixture. Coat the meat well.

3 Cover with cling film and put in the refrigerator overnight.

4 The next day, put the meat in a non-metallic baking dish. Add 500ml lamb stock and bake in a preheated oven at 180°C/350°F/Gas Mark 4 for 2 hours. Turn from time to time, basting with the marinade so that the meat acquires a delicious glaze. If the meat is too brown on the outside, cover with foil and continue baking.

5 Serve with boiled new potatoes, green beans and tomato and baby spinach salad.

Pork Cooked in Tomatillo Sauce
Puerco en Salsa de Tomate Verde

This dish is a tradition in Mexican homes. This recipe uses pork belly, but other cuts, such as spare ribs, are equally as good. It is best to cook this dish over a long period, so that the meat gets very tender and the tomatillo caramelizes and loses all its acidity.

PREPARATION TIME: 20 minutes / **COOKING TIME:** 1 hour 30 minutes / **SERVES:** 4

500g pork belly, cut into chunks ◆ 1 tablespoon corn or vegetable oil
1 medium onion, finely sliced ◆ 1 clove garlic, finely chopped ◆ 375ml canned tomatillos
½ teaspoon coarse salt ◆ ½ teaspoon sugar ◆ ¼ teaspoon bicarbonate of soda (to counteract
the acidity of the tomatillos) ◆ 1 sprig fresh oregano ◆ 125ml vegetable stock
4 tablespoons fresh coriander, chopped

◆

1 Preheat the oven to 180°C/350°F/Gas Mark 4.

2 Heat a large flameproof casserole dish and put in the pork belly, searing the meat until it turns golden brown. Set the meat aside. In the same dish, add the vegetable oil and onion. Sauté until the onion is soft and translucent. Add the garlic and continue cooking for a further minute.

3 Add the tomatillos, salt, sugar, bicarbonate of soda and oregano. Stir well. Add the meat and stir to coat the meat with the sauce. Bring to the boil and simmer for 10 minutes. Add some stock to thin, if necessary. Cover the dish with a tight-fitting lid or aluminium foil and cook in the centre of the oven for 1 hour. Check occasionally to make sure the dish is not too dry. Add more stock if necessary.

4 Before serving, stir in the chopped coriander.

5 Serve with Mexican-style Rice (see page 46), sautéed potatoes, Refried Beans (see page 87) and baby spinach and tomato salad.

Fish in Pomegranate Sauce
Pescado en Salsa de Granadas

Pomegranates are an import from Europe, via Spain; however, they are often used in Mexican cooking. This is an innovative recipe for fish. Use pomegranates when they are in season — in Mexico, this is from September to December.

PREPARATION TIME: 20 minutes / **COOKING TIME:** 15 minutes / **SERVES:** 6

4 large pomegranates ◆ 1 teaspoon sugar ◆ Juice of 1 lemon
1kg fish fillets (sea bass works well)
Salt and freshly ground black pepper ◆ Olive oil

◆

1 Cut the pomegranates in half and scrape out the seeds. Reserve some of the seeds to use as a garnish. Put the rest of the seeds in a food processor with the sugar and lemon juice and blend until puréed. Reserve.

2 Put a sheet of baking paper on top of a sheet of aluminum foil. Put a fish fillet on the paper and season with salt and pepper. Pour the pomegranate sauce over the fish and drizzle with oil. Close up the parcel, making sure that the edges are well sealed. Repeat the process with all of the fish pieces. Steam the parcels or bake them in a preheated oven at 180°C/350°F/Gas Mark 4 for 15 minutes or until the fillets are cooked.

3 Serve hot and garnish with the reserved pomegranate seeds. Serve with White Rice (see page 48) and a watercress salad dressed with extra virgin olive oil and a dash of lemon juice.

Mexican Fish Pie

Empanada de Pescado

My mother's very close friends Gloria and Malala Ugarte have been very keen cooks for many years and they used to share recipes, gossip and knitting patterns with my mother. Their niece Paz has become a very good friend to both my mother and me, and she very kindly sent me this recipe.

PREPARATION TIME: 30 minutes / **COOKING TIME:** 1 hour / **SERVES:** 6

1 tablespoon butter, softened ◆ 1kg packet shortcrust or puff pastry
350g cod fillets ◆ ¼ onion, chopped ◆ 1 bay leaf ◆ Pinch of salt
2 tablespoons extra virgin olive oil ◆ 1 medium onion, finely chopped
3 cloves garlic, finely chopped ◆ 4 large ripe tomatoes, peeled and finely chopped,
or use 400g canned chopped tomatoes ◆ Pinch of sugar ◆ 1 teaspoon dried oregano
2 tablespoons fresh parsley, finely chopped ◆ 10 green olives, stoned and finely chopped
20 capers in brine, drained and finely chopped ◆ Salt and pepper ◆ 1 large egg, beaten

◆

1 Grease a 20 x 20cm ovenproof dish with the butter.

2 Divide the pastry in half. Set aside one half. Roll out half to a square 5cm larger than the ovenproof dish. Fit inside the dish, making sure it covers all sides of the dish. The reserved pastry half will form the lid of the Empanada.

3 Poach the fish fillets for 4 minutes in a little water containing the ¼ chopped onion, the bay leaf and salt. Remove and leave to cool.

4 Prepare the sauce by sautéing the remaining onion for about 5 minutes in the olive oil, until soft and translucent. Add the garlic and cook for a further 2 minutes, stirring constantly. Add the tomatoes and sugar and continue cooking for 5 minutes or until the sauce thickens. Add the oregano and parsley.

5 Flake the fish with your fingers and add to the tomato sauce. Add the chopped olives and capers and stir. Taste and adjust the seasonings.

6 Preheat the oven to 180°C/350°F/Gas Mark 4. Put the fish and tomato mixture into the pastry-lined dish. Roll out the reserved pastry and use to cover and seal the edges of the filling. Brush with a little beaten egg.

7 Cook in the centre of the preheated oven for 40 minutes, until the pastry is cooked and golden.

8 The Empanada can be served hot or cold with watercress, baby spinach and spring onion salad.

Tuna and Crab Salpicón Salad
Salpicón de Jaiba y Atún

This is a delicious salad that is very refreshing on a hot day. Use good-quality fresh tuna and crabmeat.

PREPARATION TIME: 15 minutes / **COOKING TIME:** 5 minutes / **SERVES:** 6–8

200g fresh tuna steaks ◆ 150g fresh crabmeat, cooked and shredded ◆ ½ red onion, finely sliced, soaked in water and drained ◆ 2 ripe plum tomatoes, chopped
1 large ripe avocado, cut into wedges ◆ 4 heads cos lettuce, thickly sliced
4 tablespoons extra virgin olive oil ◆ 1 tablespoon lime juice ◆ ¼ teaspoon dried oregano
2 tablespoons fresh coriander, finely chopped ◆ Salt and pepper

◆

1 Heat a heavy-based frying pan. Fry the tuna for 1 minute on each side. Remove from the frying pan and slice thinly. Reserve.

2 In a large salad bowl, place the crabmeat, red onion, tomatoes, avocado and lettuce. Pour over the olive oil, lime juice, oregano, coriander, salt and pepper and toss by hand to mix. Add the tuna slices to the salad and toss gently.

3 Serve in a large salad bowl and allow guests to help themselves.

Veracruz-style Fish
Pescado a la Veracruzana

My maternal grandmother was born and educated in Cordoba, in the state of Veracruz. This dish is a speciality of that state and the use of olives and capers is an example of the Spanish influence on Mexican shores. Again, we see the marriage of cultures in this dish with the addition of chillies.

PREPARATION TIME: 20 minutes / **COOKING TIME:** 25 minutes / **SERVES:** 6

2 tablespoons olive oil ◆ 1 medium onion, finely sliced ◆ 3 cloves garlic, pounded with some salt into a paste ◆ 500g canned chopped plum tomatoes
1 green pepper, finely sliced ◆ 1 yellow pepper, finely sliced
1 red pepper, finely sliced ◆ 1 teaspoon dried oregano ◆ 2 bay leaves
85g capers in brine, drained and rinsed ◆ 150g plain green olives, sliced
170g fresh white fish ◆ 4 Greek or Spanish yellow peppers in brine

◆

1 Heat the oil in a frying pan. Sauté the onions until soft. Add the garlic paste and cook for a further 2 minutes. Add the tomatoes, sliced peppers, oregano and bay leaves. Cook for about 10 minutes, stirring so that the sauce does not stick to the frying pan. Add the capers and olives.

2 Preheat the oven to 180°C/350°F/Gas Mark 4.

3 Season the fish and broil it in a pan with a little oil, until golden in colour.

4 Place half of the sauce in a baking dish and add the fish. Pour over the remaining sauce.

Cover with foil and bake in the preheated oven for 15 minutes. If using a whole fish, bake for a little longer.

5 Before serving, add the canned yellow peppers. Serve with plain white rice and a green salad.

Mama says...
It's traditional to use whole red snapper in this dish, but any white fish with a firm flesh would work just as well.

Poblano Peppers Filled with Tuna
Chiles Poblanos Rellenos de Atun

Poblano chillies are abundant in Mexico; we eat them in the same way people of other countries eat peppers. We stuff them with a variety of fillings. I have chosen a filling that's perfect for the summertime. In season in July and August, poblanos can be hot or mild – either way, they are delicious. Don't be scared to try poblanos: they are full of flavour, especially when they have been chargrilled or roasted.

PREPARATION TIME: 35 minutes / **COOKING TIME:** 15 minutes / **SERVES:** 4

4 poblano chillies ◆ 300g canned tuna in oil, drained and crumbled into large chunks
1 cup red onion, finely chopped, plus extra to garnish
1 large ripe tomato, finely chopped ◆ 1 sprig fresh oregano (tear the leaves and roughly chop), plus extra to garnish ◆ 2 tablespoons white wine vinegar, plus extra for drizzling
4 tablespoons extra virgin olive oil, plus extra for drizzling ◆ Salt and pepper

◆

1 Start by preparing the chillies. Carefully burn their skins on the hob or under a grill, turning them from time to time until blackened all over. Put them in a plastic bag and wrap in a tea towel.

2 In a large bowl, prepare the filling by mixing together the tuna, red onion, tomato, oregano, white wine vinegar and olive oil. Season to taste with salt and pepper.

3 Once the chillies are cool, remove from the bag. Use a tea towel or a blunt knife to peel off the burnt skin. Wearing rubber gloves, cut a slit lengthways and carefully remove the seeds.

4 Stuff the chillies with the tuna mix. Substitute the tuna with crumbled feta cheese if cooking for vegetarians.

5 Serve the chillies on a bed of colourful lettuce and garnish with red onion and oregano leaves. Drizzle some oil and vinegar over the top before serving.

Auntie Mercedes's
Cheese and Poblano Cake
Pastel de Queso de la Tía Mercedes

Auntie Mercedes was my mother's aunt and another great cook. She used to run a small catering business in Mexico City and was well known for her baking. She traditionally made the cakes and pastries for every family party. I don't remember a lot about her except that she had a lovely smile, she was always happy and her immaculate house smelled of butter and baking. This recipe is good to serve as part of a buffet for a party.

PREPARATION TIME: 20 minutes / **COOKING TIME:** 30 minutes / **SERVES:** 6–8

110g butter ◆ 100g sugar ◆ 2 large eggs ◆ 1 egg white ◆ 100g plain flour
1 teaspoon baking powder ◆ 500g feta cheese, crumbled ◆ 1 tablespoon soured cream
170g jar Spanish piquillo red peppers in oil or brine, drained
2 poblano peppers, deseeded, deveined and thinly sliced
100g grated cheddar cheese

◆

1 Beat together the butter and sugar until creamy. Add the eggs and egg white and continue beating. Add the flour, baking powder, crumbled feta and soured cream.

2 Grease a ring mould. Pour half of the mixture into the base of the mould and cover with most of the piquillo peppers. Cover this layer with the cheddar cheese and the poblano peppers. Cover with the rest of the egg and cheese mixture.

3 Preheat the oven to 180°C/350°F/Gas Mark 4. Place the mould in the preheated oven for 30 minutes. Once cooked, remove from the oven and leave to cool for about 5 minutes. Turn out the mould on to a large platter and garnish with the remaining piquillo peppers, sliced thinly.

Seviche Tostadas

Tostadas de Ceviche

Seviche, raw fish marinated in lime juice, is eaten throughout Latin America. It is delicious served on crispy tostadas. Be sure to use the freshest fish possible and keep it cold at all times. Try using different fish: tuna, salmon and sea bass are all very good in this recipe.

PREPARATION TIME: 20 minutes / **MARINATING TIME:** 4 hours
COOKING TIME: 15 minutes / **MAKES:** 12 tostadas

750g fleshy fish (use sea bass, red snapper or tuna steaks or a mixture of fish)
400ml fresh lime juice ◆ 1 large red onion, finely chopped ◆ 1 clove garlic, finely chopped
400g canned chopped plum tomatoes or ripe tomatoes
1 bunch fresh coriander, finely chopped ◆ 2 serrano or bird's-eye chillies, finely chopped
30g green olives (optional) ◆ Salt and freshly ground black pepper
4 tablespoons olive oil ◆ 12 soft corn tortillas ◆ 80ml corn or vegetable oil
2 avocados, cut into wedges

◆

1 Place the fish in a glass bowl and add the lime juice. Cover and refrigerate for 4 hours, until the fish has 'cooked' in the lime juice. One way to test it is to see that it has changed colour and that it is firmer in texture.

2 Mix together the red onion, garlic, tomatoes, coriander, chillies and olives. Season with salt and pepper. Taste frequently and adjust the seasonings. Drain the fish and mix into the sauce.

3 Heat the oil in a medium-sized frying pan and fry the tortillas until golden brown and crisp. Remove from the frying pan, put on kitchen paper to absorb excess oil and leave to cool.

4 Put a serving of seviche on each tostada and garnish with avocado slices. Serve as a snack with tequila shots or beer.

Mama says...
If the seviche is not 'tomatoey' enough, add some ketchup.

chapter four

Frijoles, Papas & Ensladas

BEANS, POTATOES & SALADS

Back Burner Beans

Frijoles de la Olla

These beans are a staple in most Mexican homes. You'll always find a pot of cooked or cooking beans at the back of the hob. They are nutritious and versatile – they can be used as a base to make other recipes, such as refried beans, bean salad or bean soup.

PREPARATION TIME: 10 minutes, plus overnight soaking / **COOKING TIME:** 1 hour 30 minutes
SERVES: 6

400g dried pinto, borlotti or black beans ◆ 2 litres water
1 large onion, quartered ◆ 3 whole cloves garlic ◆ 2 bay leaves
1 small bunch fresh mixed herbs ◆ Salt

◆

1 Soak the beans in the water overnight. The next day, transfer them to a large saucepan of water and bring to the boil. Skim off any film that comes to the surface. Add the onions, garlic, bay leaves and herbs. Partially cover and simmer gently for about 1 hour or until the beans are fully cooked and soft. Once cooked, season with salt.

2 Serve as an accompaniment to other dishes. Try serving as a soup with a squeeze of lime juice and a dash of hot pepper sauce, some Pico de Gallo (see page 100), soured cream and warm Tortillas (see page 20).

Refried Beans
Frijoles Refritos

This must be the most famous Mexican bean dish. Serve them at lunch to accompany a main course. They are very easy to make.

PREPARATION TIME: 15 minutes / **COOKING TIME:** 10 minutes / **SERVES:** 4–6

**2 cups Frijoles de la Olla (see page 86) with a little cooking water, or the same quantity of canned borlotti, cannellini, black or pinto beans, rinsed and drained
1 medium onion, finely chopped ◆ 1 tablespoon corn or vegetable oil
Salt or vegetable bouillon powder**

1 Lightly mash the beans with a potato masher until they form a soft and lumpy paste.

2 Sauté the onion and oil in a medium-sized frying pan until translucent, add the beans and cook for a further 2 minutes. Add water or bean stock if the mixture is too dry. Season with salt or vegetable bouillon powder to taste.

3 Serve as a side dish with crumbled feta cheese and tortilla chips to garnish, or use as an ingredient for *molletes* (see 'Mama says').

Mama says...
Try making molletes: take a loaf of French bread and cut in half. spread with refried beans, top with grated cheddar cheese, put under a grill and serve with Pico de Gallo (see page 100) or salsa Molcajeteada (see page 110). Try adding fried diced chorizo or crisp diced bacon before adding the cheese.

Country Beans with Chorizo
Frijoles Charros con Chorizo

These beans are served as part of a Mexican breakfast buffet or as a bean course after the main course at lunch.

PREPARATION TIME: 20 minutes / **COOKING TIME:** 15 minutes / **SERVES:** 4–6

2 chorizo sausages, diced ◆ 1 medium onion, finely chopped ◆ 2 cloves garlic, finely chopped ◆ 1 serrano or bird's-eye chilli, finely chopped ◆ 1 tablespoon tomato purée
500ml Frijoles de la Olla with stock (see page 86)

◆

1 Heat a deep, heavy-based frying pan and add the chorizo sausage. Sauté until golden brown. Remove and drain on kitchen paper.

2 Use the chorizo fat to sauté the onion and garlic until soft. Add the serrano chilli.

Cook for a further 2 minutes. Add the tomato purée and beans with the stock. Cook for 10 minutes, until the sauce thickens.

3 Serve warm in small individual bowls.

Bean, Corn, Avocado and Salsa Salad

Ensalada de Frijoles, Maíz y Aguacates

This is a really refreshing salad – perfect for outdoor lunches and versatile enough to be served with any type of meat or fish.

PREPARATION TIME: 20 minutes / **SERVES:** 6

500ml Frijoles de la Olla (see page 86) or the same quantity canned black or borlotti beans, or a mixture, rinsed and drained
250g canned corn, drained ◆ 6 ripe tomatoes, quartered
1 red onion, finely sliced ◆ 2 tablespoons fresh coriander, chopped
1 serrano or bird's-eye chilli, finely sliced ◆ 80ml olive oil ◆ 50ml cider vinegar
Salt and pepper ◆ 4 ripe avocados

◆

1 In a large bowl, mix together the beans, corn, tomatoes, red onion, coriander and chilli with your hands. Add the oil, vinegar, salt and pepper. Mix well.

2 Place on a colourful serving dish and add the slices of avocado just before serving. Serve with Seviche (see page 82).

Cactus Salad

Ensalada de Nopales

This is my version of ensalada de nopales, which is served on a variety of corn snacks in Mexican markets and is delicious in its own right. I tend to chop the ingredients larger than they would in Mexico and it looks very colourful. Eating cactus can raise eyebrows, but people are always converted after tasting this salad.

PREPARATION TIME: 25 minutes / **COOKING TIME:** 15 minutes / **SERVES:** 6

1kg freshly cooked cactus, sliced ◆ 500g ripe fresh tomatoes, cut into wedges
1 red onion, finely chopped ◆ 1 tablespoon dried oregano
60ml white wine vinegar ◆ 215ml olive oil
500g diced feta cheese ◆ 2 tablespoons fresh coriander, finely chopped
Salt and pepper

◆

1 In a large bowl, mix together the cactus, tomatoes, red onion, oregano, vinegar, oil, feta cheese, coriander and salt and pepper with your hands.

2 Serve with tostadas, guacamole and a tequila aperitif.

Mama says...
Try to use fresh cactus (nopales), which can be found ready-peeled in Mexican markets. Cook in salted water with oregano and half an onion. The onion will keep the cactus from turning slimy. Cook until soft in the centre. If using canned cactus, drain and rinse thoroughly.

Grilled Peppers and Mushrooms in Soured Cream

Rajas y Champiñones con Crema

These can be served as a side dish instead of (or as well as) refried beans, but they are also a delicious addition at any taco party.

PREPARATION TIME: 30 minutes / **COOKING TIME:** 20 minutes / **SERVES:** 6–8

5 poblano peppers or green peppers ◆ 2 tablespoons corn oil
2 medium onions, finely sliced ◆ 500g mushrooms (add wild mushrooms
such as porcini or shiitake if possible) ◆ 200ml soured cream ◆ Salt and pepper

◆

1 Wash the peppers and dry them with kitchen paper. Place them either under the grill or in the flame on the hob. Turn them, burning the skins until they are blackened. Place them inside a plastic bag and wrap with a tea towel. Leave them to steam for about 5 minutes.

2 Remove the peppers from the bag and leave to cool. Peel off the blackened skins and slice the peppers into strips.

3 Heat the oil in a heavy-based frying pan. Fry the sliced onion in the oil, and when soft and caramelized, about 10 minutes, add the mushrooms and cook until soft. Add the grilled peppers and stir well.

4 Remove from the heat and leave to cool for about 2 minutes. Add the soured cream gradually, stirring constantly. Season with salt and pepper. Serve with warm flour tortillas as a snack.

Cucumber, Cumin and Mint Salad
Ensalada de Pepinos, Comino y Hierbabuena

I don't think that this salad is strictly Mexican, but it is a salad that my mum used to make when I was a child and works wonderfully with most Mexican dishes. Buy the freshest ingredients possible and enjoy its refreshing flavour.

PREPARATION TIME: 15 minutes / **SERVES:** 4

**2 large cucumbers, peeled and deseeded ◆ 4 spring onions, sliced
60ml olive oil ◆ 2 tablespoons white wine vinegar
½ teaspoon ground cumin or roasted cumin seeds
Handful fresh mint, chopped ◆ Salt and black pepper**

1 Cut the peeled and deseeded cucumbers in half. Dry with kitchen paper, slice and lay out on a large serving dish.

2 Put the spring onions, olive oil, vinegar, cumin, mint and salt and pepper in a clean, empty jar. Screw the lid on tightly and shake well to mix the ingredients.

3 Pour the mixture over the cucumber. This salad improves if left for a while to absorb the flavours before serving. Serve at room temperature.

Coriander Pesto
Salsa de Cilantro del Ranchito

Of course, this is not pesto in the strict sense. It is really caramelized onions with lots of coriander and is fantastic served with waxy new potatoes. Try to find fresh coriander, sold in bunches at many supermarkets with the roots still attached, as this is the best coriander you can buy.

PREPARATION TIME: 25 minutes / **COOKING TIME:** 15 minutes / **MAKES:** 1 large jar

**300g unsalted butter ◆ 2 large onions, finely chopped
3 large bunches fresh coriander, finely chopped ◆ Salt and pepper**

1 Heat the butter in a pan. Add the onions and sauté for 10 minutes, until caramelized. Remove from the heat, add the coriander and stir. Season to taste with salt and pepper.

2 Store in the refrigerator for up to 1 week. This recipe can be halved or quartered in quantity without altering the final result.

New Potatoes with Coriander Pesto
Papas con Cilantro del Ranchito

This was a signature dish at our favourite taco restaurant, El Ranchito in Coyoacan. They used to serve these potatoes in small clay pots.

PREPARATION TIME: 10 minutes / **COOKING TIME:** 15 minutes / **SERVES:** 6

**1kg baby new potatoes
1 jar Coriander Pesto (see recipe above)**

1 Wash the potatoes. Put them in a large saucepan of water and bring to a boil. Cook the potatoes until soft. Drain.

2 In a large bowl, mix together the coriander pesto and potatoes so they are thoroughly coated.

3 Serve with the dish of your choice.

Potatoes with Tomatoes, Coriander and Chilli
Papas con Jitomates, Cilantro y Chilito

This dish is ideal for using up leftover potatoes and is eaten as a hangover cure or a winter 'pick-me-up'. Perfect as a dish to accompany most meals, the kick of chilli combined with the fragrant aroma of coriander is really tasty.

PREPARATION TIME: 30 minutes / **COOKING TIME:** 20 minutes / **SERVES:** 4

**1kg baby new potatoes ◆ 2 tablespoons vegetable oil
500g Salsa Molcajeteada (see page 110) or Pico de Gallo (see page 100)**

1 Wash the potatoes. Chop into smaller pieces if they are a little large. Bring a large saucepan of water to the boil and cook the potatoes until soft, about 10 minutes. Drain and reserve.

2 Heat the oil in a frying pan. Sauté the salsa for about 2 minutes. Add the potatoes to the frying pan and mix until coated in the salsa.

3 Serve with any meat of your choice.

*Mama says...
This dish is perfect for serving at barbecues.*

Fried Plantains
Platanos Machos Fritos

Fried plantains are widely eaten in the tropical parts of Mexico, such as Veracruz and Tabasco. They are also eaten in the Caribbean. Plantains are usually served on top of white rice or as a side dish.

PREPARATION TIME: 10 minutes / **COOKING TIME:** 15 minutes / **SERVES:** 6

220g butter
2 ripe plantains, cut into 1cm slices diagonally or lengthways

◆

1 Clarify the butter by heating it gently in a saucepan. Separate the clear butter from the solids by straining.

2 Heat the clear butter and add the plantain slices, one by one, taking care that they don't get stuck to each other. Fry them gently, until soft and golden all over.

3 Remove from the pan and place on kitchen paper to absorb the excess butter. Serve warm as a side dish.

Mama says...
The riper the plantains, the better the results. A really ripe plantain will have a skin that is mostly black. Although this might look unsightly, it is in fact desirable.

chapter five
Salsas
SAUCES

Mexican Salsa

Salsa Mexicana tipo Pico de Gallo

This is the simplest of salsas and it can be turned into things such as Seviche (see page 82), a base for a Mexican prawn cocktail, guacamole or a base for Cactus Salad (see page 90). It is so versatile and is a staple of Mexican cuisine.

PREPARATION TIME: 15 minutes / **MAKES:** 1 medium bowl

**1 medium red onion, finely chopped ◆ 4 large tomatoes, chopped
Half bunch fresh coriander, finely chopped ◆ 1–2 fresh serrano or bird's-eye chillies,
finely chopped ◆ Salt and pepper ◆ Juice of ½ lime**

1 In a large bowl, combine the onion, tomatoes, coriander and chillies. Add the salt, pepper and lime juice to taste. Pound with a pestle and mortar if you prefer a fine-textured salsa.

2 Experiment with other ingredients. Add sliced avocados, prawns, cooked cactus or feta to the salsa. The variations are endless!

Mama says...
Try grilling the tomatoes and chillies until charred. This will give a delicious roasted flavour to the salsa.

Tomatillo Salsa

Salsa de Tomates Verdes

The tomatillo is a fruit that belongs to the same family as physalis. They are very pretty and come in their own natural casing. Many call them green tomatoes because that is exactly what they look like, but they are not actually related to tomatoes – they never turn red. Tomatillos are very acidic and they need to be cooked before eating. In some parts of Europe, they are available in cans, but this is not as desirable as using fresh tomatillos.

PREPARATION TIME: 20 minutes / COOKING TIME: 15 minutes / MAKES: 1 medium bowl

**1 tablespoon corn or vegetable oil ◆ ½ medium onion, finely chopped
1 clove garlic, crushed ◆ 200g fresh tomatillos (or 250g canned tomatillo purée)
2 serrano or bird's-eye chillies, finely chopped ◆ 2 tablespoons fresh coriander, finely chopped ◆ ½ teaspoon salt ◆ ½ teaspoon sugar ◆ ¼ teaspoon bicarbonate of soda
(to counteract the acidity of the tomatillos)**

◆

1 In a medium-sized saucepan, heat the oil and add the onion. Sauté for 5 minutes, until soft. Add the garlic and sauté for a further 2 minutes, making sure the garlic does not burn.

2 Add the tomatillo purée, chilli, coriander, salt, sugar and bicarbonate of soda. Cook for 10 minutes, until the sauce tastes less acidic.

Mama says...
Give this salsa a twist by adding some puréed ripe avocado and mixing well. The salsa will taste richer, creamier and milder.

Habanero Salsa
Salsa de Chile Habanero

The habanero is the hottest chilli around and it grows in the Yucatan area and in the Caribbean. Although it is very hot, it is also very tasty. This salsa should be eaten sparingly. Just a little habanero chilli added to a dish will give it plenty of heat and flavour.

PREPARATION TIME: 15 minutes / **COOKING TIME:** 15 minutes / **MAKES:** 1 jar

**2 red onions, finely chopped ◆ 2 tablespoons orange juice
1 tablespoon cider vinegar ◆ 1 habanero chilli, finely sliced
Salt and pepper**

◆

1 In a bowl, mix together the red onion, orange juice, vinegar, chilli, salt and pepper.

2 Put the salsa into an empty, clean jar and screw on the lid tightly. Preserve the salsa by adding a layer of olive oil to the surface of the salsa. Store in the refrigerator for up to 2 weeks.

Mama says...
important note: Be very careful when preparing this chilli. Use rubber gloves when handling, if possible.

Red Onion and Habanero Relish
Jalea de Habanero y Cebolla Roja

This is a relish that is both sweet and hot. It is a bit like marmalade but with a far more powerful kick! Serve as a chutney with fish and meat dishes.

PREPARATION TIME: 15 minutes / **COOKING TIME:** 15 minutes / **MAKES:** 1 jar

3 tablespoons olive oil ◆ 5 red onions, chopped
1 tablespoon black treacle ◆ 1 teaspoon finely diced habanero chilli
(see 'Mama says' on page 103) ◆ Juice of 1 orange
1 tablespoon cider vinegar ◆ ½ teaspoon coarse salt

1 Heat the oil in a frying pan. Add the onion and treacle and sauté the onions until caramelized.

2 Add the chilli, orange juice, vinegar and salt. Cook for about 3 minutes to reduce. The consistency should be similar to marmalade.

Saturday Guacamole
Guacamole del Sábado

This is a simple recipe that my father used to prepare each Saturday to serve with aperitifs. Neighbours and relatives would pop by and nibble on this with warm tortillas and other snacks.

PREPARATION TIME: 20 minutes / **MAKES:** 1 medium bowl

2 ripe avocados ◆ Juice of ½ lime ◆ 1 medium onion, chopped
4 large tomatoes, chopped ◆ 2 tablespoons fresh coriander, finely chopped
1–2 fresh serrano or bird's-eye chillies, finely chopped
Salt and freshly ground black pepper

1 In a bowl, mash the avocados lightly to form a rough, lumpy purée. Add the lime juice and combine.

2 In another bowl, mix together the onion, tomatoes, coriander and chillies. Add the avocado and lime mixture. Stir well to incorporate. Season to taste with salt and freshly ground black pepper and serve.

Guajillo Chilli Salsa
Salsa de Chile Guajillo

The guajillo chilli is a friendly chilli that tastes quite mild. It is the base for a number of dishes. Here, it makes a delicious salsa that tastes good accompanied by any food, as it is not hot or overpowering in any way.

PREPARATION TIME: 10 minutes / **MAKES:** 1 medium bowl

3 dried guajillo chillies, deveined and deseeded ◆ **125ml hot water**
3 whole cloves garlic, unpeeled ◆ **2 tablespoons roughly chopped onion** ◆ **½ teaspoon salt**

◆

1 Prepare the chillies and cut into medium-sized chunks. Put in the small compartment of a food processor – the section used to grind spices. Add a little hot water.

2 Heat a heavy-based frying pan and roast the garlic cloves until soft. Peel and add to the food processor along with the onion and salt. Blend well until a purée is formed. Serve.

Mama says...
Add a little orange juice to give this salsa a twist.

Drunken Salsa

Salsa Borracha

This salsa can be quite fiery and is very good served with grilled meats. It is especially delicious served with Carne al Pastor (see page 124). It contains pasilla chillies, which are fairly hot. The addition of serrano or bird's-eye chillies make this salsa even more fiery.

PREPARATION TIME: 15 minutes / **MAKES:** 1 medium bowl

100g dried pasilla chillies ♦ 250ml hot water ♦ 80ml fresh orange juice
2 cloves garlic, finely chopped ♦ 1 tablespoon cider vinegar ♦ 1 large onion, finely chopped
1 serrano or bird's-eye chilli, finely chopped ♦ ¼ teaspoon black treacle
½ teaspoon salt ♦ Pinch of dried thyme ♦ Pinch of dried oregano

1 Soak the deveined and deseeded pasilla chillies in the hot water. Remove from the water and put into the small compartment of a food processor, the section used to grind spices. Reserve the water.

2 Add the orange juice, garlic and vinegar to the food processor. Blend until a purée is formed. If the mixture is too thick, add a little of the reserved water.

3 Transfer to a bowl and add the onion, chopped serrano chilli, treacle, salt, thyme and oregano.

4 This salsa can be stored for up to 3 days in the refrigerator.

Pickled Jalapeños
Chiles Jalapeños en Vinagre

Pickled jalapeños are very popular in Mexico – they are an integral part of a Mexican torta (submarine sandwich). They go very well with roasted chicken, and are served every day at lunchtime. Pickled jalapeños contain vegetables that soak up the flavour of the chillies and herbs – these taste just as good as the jalapeños. You can also try adding a little of the pickled vinegar to soups or bean dishes.

PREPARATION TIME: 20 minutes / **COOKING TIME:** 30 minutes / **MAKES:** 1 large jar

125ml olive oil ◆ 6 whole cloves garlic, peeled ◆ 5 shallots, halved
3 large carrots, sliced ◆ 5 cauliflower florets ◆ 15 jalapeño chillies, halved
1 courgette, sliced ◆ 500ml cider vinegar or white wine vinegar ◆ 180ml water
1 sprig dried thyme ◆ 1 sprig dried oregano ◆ 6 bay leaves ◆ 1 teaspoon salt
5 black peppercorns

◆

1 In a large, heavy-based saucepan, heat the oil and sauté the garlic and shallots for 3 minutes. Add the carrots and cauliflower florets and sauté for a further 3 minutes. Add the chillies and courgette and sauté for a further 3 minutes.

2 Add the vinegar, water, thyme, oregano, bay leaves, salt and peppercorns to the pan and bring the mixture to the boil. Simmer gently for 10 minutes. Transfer to an empty, clean jar. Store in the refrigerator for up to 2 months.

Chipotles in Adobo Sauce
Chipotles en Adobo

As you can see from previous recipes, these chillies are not only served as a condiment – they are useful for imparting a very good flavour to a number of dishes. They can also be used in many other types of cuisine. I find that they lend another dimension to an Italian ragù and they make a great pizza topping. They can be stored in the refrigerator for up to 2 months. This is a recipe taken from my mother's aunts, Refugio and Mercedes, that I found in a very old family recipe book.

PREPARATION TIME: 15 minutes / **COOKING TIME:** 40 minutes / **MAKES:** 750ml

**140g dried chipotle chillies ◆ 80ml corn oil
1 medium onion, finely chopped ◆ 5 cloves garlic, finely chopped ◆ 5 bay leaves
1 sprig fresh oregano, finely chopped ◆ 1 sprig fresh thyme, finely chopped
625ml cider vinegar ◆ 1 tablespoon orange juice ◆ 375ml water
1½ teaspoons salt ◆ 5 tablespoons black treacle**

1 Rinse the chillies. Make an incision in the chillies with a sharp knife and reserve.

2 In a heavy-based saucepan, heat the oil and sauté the onion for about 2 minutes. Add the garlic and sauté for a further minute. Add the chillies and sauté for a further 5 minutes.

3 Add the bay leaves, oregano, thyme, vinegar, orange juice, water, salt and treacle to the pan and bring the mixture to the boil. Simmer over a low heat for 25 minutes, stirring occasionally.

4 Transfer the mixture to an empty, clean glass jar. Eat immediately or leave to marinate in the refrigerator for up to 5 days for a better flavour.

5 These can be stored in the refrigerator for up to 3 months.

Pounded Chilli, Tomato and Garlic
Salsa Molcajeteada de Chilies, Jitomates y Ajo

A molcajete is an indigenous pestle and mortar made of volcanic stone. If you don't happen to possess such an item, use a blender, although it will lack that Mexican authenticity!

PREPARATION TIME: 15 minutes / **COOKING TIME:** 15 minutes / **MAKES:** 1 medium bowl

3 large ripe tomatoes ◆ **5 serrano or bird's-eye chillies**
2 whole cloves garlic, unpeeled ◆ **1 teaspoon coarse salt**

◆

1 Make a small incision in the form of a cross at the base of the tomatoes. Preheat the grill until it is very hot. Grill the chillies, garlic, and tomatoes. The garlic is ready when it is soft inside. Place this in the molcajete or blender. The chillies will blacken and are ready when soft. Remove the tops, chop finely and add to the molcajete or blender with the garlic. Remove the seeds if you prefer a milder salsa, or leave them if you like it hot! Add the salt to the garlic and chillies and pound or blend until it becomes a paste.

2 The tomatoes will need longer to grill. They need to be blackened all over and quite soft. Remove from the heat and peel, chop roughly and put in the molcajete or blender. Pound or blend the tomatoes together with the garlic and chilli paste. The mixture should remain slightly lumpy.

3 Serve in a large serving dish and allow guests to help themselves. This salsa is very hot, but absolutely delicious.

Mama says...
This salsa will store well for up to a week in the refrigerator.

Jalapeños Marinated with Limes
Rajas de Jalapeño con Limón

This is a fiery but delicious mixture that is often served with steaks at barbecues. Barbecued spring onions taste excellent when sprinkled with some of this marinating juice.

PREPARATION TIME: 10 minutes / **MARINATING TIME:** 4 hours
COOKING TIME: 15 minutes / **MAKES:** 1 medium bowl

6 whole jalapeño peppers ◆ **1 tablespoon vegetable oil** ◆ **1 onion, finely sliced**
Juice of 1 lime ◆ **2 tablespoons soy sauce mixed with 2 tablespoons Worcestershire sauce**

◆

1 Preheat the grill. Grill the jalapeños until soft. Remove from the heat. Remove the tops with a sharp knife, discard the seeds and slice lengthways.

2 Heat the oil in a frying pan and sauté the onion for 10 minutes, until soft and caramelized.

3 In an empty, clean glass jar, mix the lime juice with the two sauces. Add the grilled jalapeños and onions. Mix well and leave to marinate for about 3 hours before serving.

4 Store in the refrigerator for up to 1 week.

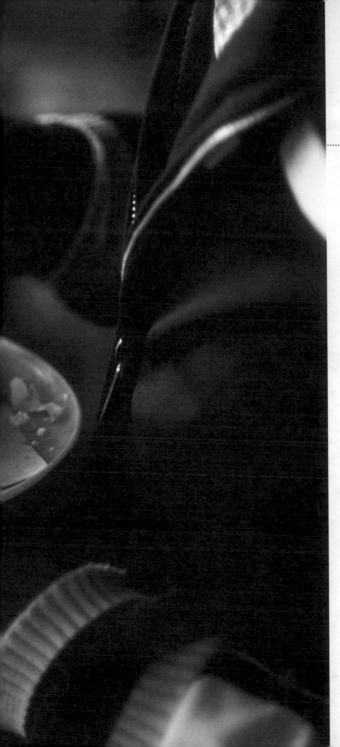

chapter six

Antojitos
EVENING SNACKS

Enchiladas from San Luis Potosi
Enchiladas Potosinas

These are not enchiladas as you know them; they are called 'enchiladas' because they are made with fresh maize dough and chilli. These vegetarian enchiladas are filled with feta cheese and are very good served as finger food. They are made with ancho chilli, which is not hot, but gives flavour and colour. So here is a recipe to dispel the myth that chillies, and therefore Mexican food, are just unbearably hot. The enchiladas can be made in a large batch in advance and then frozen. To reheat later, simply put them in the oven until warm. Serve them with salad and salsa.

PREPARATION TIME: 30 minutes / **COOKING TIME:** 30 minutes / **MAKES:** 26

1 medium dried ancho chilli, deseeded ◆ 500ml hot water ◆ 375g masa harina
½ teaspoon salt ◆ 1 large onion, finely chopped
250ml corn oil, for frying ◆ 300g crumbled feta cheese

1 Cut the chili into large chunks. You can do this with scissors or with your fingers. Be careful when dealing with chillies: some can be hot, so it is best to wear rubber gloves. Add 250ml of the hot water and leave for a few minutes to infuse. Purée in a blender until you get a smooth paste. It should be dark in colour and fairly thick.

2 Put the masa harina into a mixing bowl (you can do this with a machine or by hand). Add the chilli paste, the salt and the rest of the water. Mix until fully incorporated and the *masa* (dough) resembles marzipan. Leave to rest for a few minutes.

3 Caramelize the onion in 2 tablespoons of the oil. When soft and brown, mix with the feta. This is the filling.

4 Make the tortillas by taking a small ball of the dough and placing it between two sheets of cling film. Flatten with a rolling pin or with a tortilla press if you have one. You are aiming for a tortilla that is about 7cm in diameter.

5 Peel the tortilla from the cling film and fill with about 1 tablespoon of the filling, placing it in the centre across the tortilla. Fold the tortilla over. It should now resemble a half-moon with the filling on one side of the enchilada.

6 Repeat the process, and when you have finished, heat the remaining oil in a large frying pan. When the oil is hot and starting to smoke, slide 3–4 of the enchiladas carefully into the oil and leave them to cook for about 2 minutes on each side. Control the heat so that they fry gently. They will turn darker in colour and become crispy. When they are crisp on both sides, place on kitchen paper so that the excess oil is absorbed.

7 Serve on a bed of lettuce and eat with guacamole or salsa on top. These enchiladas can be served hot or cold. To reheat, simply place on a baking sheet and heat in the oven at 150°C/300°F/Gas Mark 2 for 5 minutes. They are perfect as starters or as finger food.

Tamales

Tamales

Tamales are steamed corn dumplings that are sold all over the country. In every village, town and city, you will find people selling steaming tamales from stalls, usually outside churches, where they entice patrons with their irresistible flavour and distract them from their prayers. Some people have mobile stalls, a contraption attached to the front of a bicycle that holds a steamer full of ready-to-eat tamales; they cycle down the street shouting out their wares. The smell of a tamale is evocative of many moments and celebrations, because tamales are festive foods too, served at christenings, on the Day of the Dead and even at weddings.

PREPARATION TIME: 1 hour / **COOKING TIME:** 2 hours / **MAKES:** approximately 27

**27 corn husks ◆ 1.8kg masa harina ◆ 1½ tablespoons salt
250ml vegetable oil or 250g melted vegetable fat or lard
1 litre warm water (maybe more)**

1 Rinse off any dirt from the corn husks and soak in hot water.

2 Mix the masa with the salt in an electric mixer with a flat paddle or in a very large bowl. Add the oil and the water little by little and mix in the machine or use your fingers until the dough resembles soft marzipan.

3 Drain the corn husks.

4 Take enough dough to fill the palm of your hand, then spread it about 5mm thick along the inside of a corn husk to cover the base and sides. Leave the ends of the husk empty. These form the edges of the parcel.

5 Add the filling of your choice in the centre of the tamale. See the next page for fillings.

6 Wrap into a little parcel, first by folding the sides over each other and then by bending the top of the husk. Place in a steamer. Fill the steamer with as many tamales as will comfortably fit. Fill the base of the steamer with about 2cm of water, making sure that the water does not touch

the base of the steamer basket. If a steamer is too hot, the water will boil dry and the tamales will burn. If it is too cold, the tamales will not cook. To ensure that the steamer is at the right temperature and that it has water, put a clean coin at the base of the pan. When the water is boiling gently, the coin will rattle. If it is quiet, the steamer is not hot enough or it has run out of water. The rattling sound should be soft and constant.

7 Steam for 2 hours. A tamale is ready when you open it and the dough doesn't stick to the husk.

8 To reheat tamales, resteam them or put them in the microwave wrapped in a moist tea towel. Simply heat until the tamale is hot.

Suggestions for fillings:
Chicken in Tomatillo Salsa: one chicken breast shredded into Tomatillo Salsa (see page 102).
Pimenton Chicken (see page 56).
Meat with Chorizo and Tomatillos (see page 71).
Chicken or Vegetables in Mole Sauce (see page 136).
Grilled Peppers and Mushrooms in Soured Cream (see page 92).

NOTE: If you are making sweet tamales, add only half the amount of salt to the mixture and add 4 tablespoons of sugar, ¼ teaspoon ground cinnamon and 2 tablespoons of raisins. You can add a few drops of red food colouring to the mix so that the tamales turn pink and they can be distinguished from the savoury ones.

Guanajuato Enchiladas
Enchiladas Mineras de Guanajuato

My paternal grandmother was from the state of Guanajuato, once home to the largest silver mines in the world. Grandma used to make these enchiladas for her eleven children when they were small and I remember her making many more for all of us when I went to visit her as a little girl!

PREPARATION TIME: 20 minutes / COOKING TIME: 20 minutes / SERVES: 4

3 guajillo chillies, deveined and deseeded ◆ 125ml hot water
3 cloves garlic, whole and unpeeled
¼ onion, roughly chopped ◆ ½ teaspoon salt
80ml corn or vegetable oil for frying ◆ 12 soft corn tortillas
500g floury potatoes (e.g., King Edward), lightly mashed and seasoned with salt and pepper ◆ ½ head iceberg lettuce ◆ 200g thinly sliced radishes
2 large ripe tomatoes, sliced ◆ 100g finely crumbled feta cheese

◆

1 Prepare the chillies and cut into medium-sized chunks. Place them in a blender. Add the hot water. Grill the garlic cloves until they are soft. Peel and add to the blender with the onion and the salt. Blend until you obtain a purée. Add some water so that you have a slightly liquid sauce. Put this mixture into a medium-sized bowl.

2 Ensure that all the other ingredients are ready, as it is important that these enchiladas be made individually.

3 Heat some oil in a medium-sized saucepan and dip the corn tortillas into the oil for about 20 seconds. They need to be done one at a time. Place on kitchen paper. Dip the tortillas in the guajillo sauce and put on a plate. Cover with some of the potato filling, fold in half and repeat until you have assembled a dish of three. Top with the lettuce, radishes, tomatoes and feta. Serve with extra salsa for more flavour. These enchiladas are to be eaten at room temperature, so don't worry that they are getting cold while you prepare them.

Auntie Mariaelena's Masa Patties
Gorditas de la Tía Mariaelena

Auntie Mariaelena is a very jolly aunt who had a kindergarten, a beautiful house and made the most delicious patties. These were so memorable that even though I haven't eaten one for many years, I still remember exactly how delicious they were. The little children at the kindergarten would have one as a treat on Fridays. They are made with bone marrow, but don't let that put you off – believe me, they are just delicious. This recipe has been re-created from memory.

PREPARATION TIME: 25 minutes / **COOKING TIME:** 20 minutes / **MAKES:** approximately 15

**1 large ancho chilli, deseeded, deveined and cut into large chunks ♦ 1 litre warm water
500g bone marrow bones ♦ 500g masa harina ♦ Salt
1 tablespoon very finely chopped fresh coriander ♦ 1 medium onion, very finely chopped
250ml vegetable or corn oil for frying**

1 Soak the chilli in a bowl with 250ml of the water and leave for 5 minutes. Blend until smooth, adding more water if necessary.

2 Using a small spoon, scoop the bone marrow out of the bones and reserve.

3 In a large bowl, mix the masa harina with the salt. Add the bone marrow, blended chilli, coriander, onion and more water if necessary. Mix with your hands until you obtain a dough that is soft and pliable.

4 Pinch off a ball of dough and pat it gently between the palms of your hands so that you have a flat round about 8cm in diameter and 1cm thick.

5 Heat the oil in a frying pan. Carefully put the dough rounds in the hot oil and cook them for about 4 minutes on each side. They should turn a deep golden colour and be crisp on the outside.

6 Take out of the oil with a slotted spoon and drain. Place on kitchen paper so that any excess oil is absorbed.

7 They are delicious with any of the salsas in this book. Serve with fresh avocado slices or with Cactus Salad (see page 90).

Mole Enchiladas
Enchiladas de Mole

This recipe should really be in the main course section of this book, but sometimes if there is leftover mole in the kitchen and chicken from earlier in the day, people make enchiladas as an evening snack. Mole enchiladas are my favourite dish of all. The combination of flavours and textures from the different ingredients provides quite a contrast, and I prefer this to the traditional mole and turkey recipe. For this recipe, I use ready-made mole, so the timing and quantities reflect this.

PREPARATION TIME: 25 minutes / **COOKING TIME:** 30 minutes / **SERVES:** 4

1 boneless skinless chicken breast ◆ 750ml water
¼ onion, chopped ◆ 1 teaspoon salt ◆ 1 bay leaf
3 tablespoons corn or vegetable oil
1 teaspoon sesame oil ◆ 2 tablespoons concentrated mole paste
12 soft corn tortillas (from a supermarket or from the recipe on page 20)
2 tablespoons soured cream ◆ 2 teaspoons sesame seeds ◆ 1 small onion, sliced in rings
2 tablespoons crumbled feta cheese

◆

1 Put the chicken breast in a small saucepan and cover with the water. Add the onion, salt and bay leaf. Bring to the boil and skim off any film that comes to the surface. Boil gently for 20 minutes or until the chicken breast is cooked. Allow it to cool a bit, then shred lightly with your fingers. Reserve.

2 While the chicken is cooking, make the sauce for the enchiladas. Heat a little bit of the vegetable oil with the sesame oil in a medium

saucepan. Add the mole paste and stir. Stirring constantly, add some chicken stock or water and continue stirring until the paste turns into a sauce. You will need to add enough stock so that the texture of the mole is like that of double cream. Take off the heat and reserve.

3 Heat the rest of the oil in a frying pan and put the tortillas in one at a time. Fry for 15 seconds and place on kitchen paper. The tortillas should remain soft. Dip each tortilla in the mole sauce,

put on a large plate and fill with a little shredded chicken. Fold in half and repeat the process with the remaining tortillas. Arrange on the plates so that each person has three enchiladas. Serve garnished with a little soured cream poured over the enchiladas and sprinkle the sesame seeds, onion and cheese on top.

Mama says...
A recipe for mole can be found in the 'Desserts & Celebrations' section of this book. However, to make mole from scratch is quite labour-intensive — you will find ready-made mole at most supermarkets. This mole is of fairly high quality and can be made to taste even better if it is sautéed in sesame oil first.

Shepherd-style Meat
Carne al Pastor

In Mexico, this meat is done on kebab-type grills, so maybe this is a Mexican adaptation of the shish kebab. When I was a university student in Mexico City, the best place for shepherd's tacos was just a few streets away, so my friends and I used to go there between lectures to eat these delicious tacos. The men who made them were true craftsmen: they used to serve thin slices of this meat on freshly made tortillas with some grilled pineapple, sprinkled with fresh coriander and chopped onion and served with Salsa Borracha (see page 107). The contrast of flavours is just fabulous. These tacos were worth skipping lectures for!

PREPARATION TIME: 40 minutes / MARINATING TIME: overnight or 4 hours
COOKING TIME: 20 minutes / SERVES: 6–10

6 dried guajillo chillies, deseeded, cut into large pieces and soaked in boiling water
4 dried pasilla chillies, deseeded, cut into large pieces and soaked in boiling water
5 cloves garlic, peeled and roughly chopped
1 teaspoon dried oregano ◆ ½ teaspoon ground cumin ◆ ½ teaspoon ground cinnamon
½ teaspoon ground allspice ◆ 3 whole cloves ◆ 150ml cider vinegar
2 teaspoons brown sugar ◆ 2 teaspoons tomato purée ◆ 2kg lean pork steaks, diced
Wooden skewers ◆ 1 fresh pineapple, cut into chunks
2 large onions, cut into chunks

◆

1 Dry-fry the spices, if you wish, then grind them with the rest of the ingredients (except the meat, pineapple and onion) and turn the marinade into a paste.

2 Rub the paste over the pork steaks, place in a glass dish, cover and refrigerate overnight.

3 Cut the steaks into square chunks or thin strips. Soak the skewers in water and skewer the meat, alternating with pieces of pineapple and onion chunks. Place on the barbecue or under a hot grill until the meat is cooked. Sprinkle with freshly chopped coriander and a squeeze of lime and top with Salsa Borracha.

Tortillas in Bean Sauce and Feta Cheese
Enfrijoladas

Enfrijoladas are a very popular snack often eaten in the evening. Because most Mexican kitchens have a pot of beans at the back of the hob and there are always tortillas around, it is obvious to combine these ingredients. Furthermore, the combination of beans and tortillas is very nutritious, providing a similar quality of protein that is found in meat.

PREPARATION TIME: 15 minutes / **COOKING TIME:** 15 minutes / **SERVES:** 4

500ml home-cooked beans with their cooking liquid, or
300g canned borlotti or pinto beans plus 200ml prepared vegetable stock
2 tablespoons vegetable oil for frying
12 soft corn or wheat tortillas ◆ 125ml soured cream
2 tablespoons crumbled feta cheese
½ medium onion, very finely chopped
50g poached, shredded chicken (optional)

◆

1 Using a blender or a food processor, blend the beans with the liquid until they turn into a purée. The purée should be fairly runny, like yogurt. If it is too thick, add more stock or water. Taste and adjust the seasonings if needed.

2 Heat the oil in a medium-sized frying pan and dip the tortillas into the oil for a few seconds. Take the tortillas out of the pan and place on kitchen paper.

3 Dip the tortillas, one at a time, in the bean sauce. Fold in half or in quarters and arrange on a plate. Put three of these tortillas on each plate. Pour over any remaining sauce and spoon on some soured cream, followed by the cheese and onion. If you like, sprinkle some poached and shredded chicken on top.

chapter seven

Postres &
Días Festivos
DESSERTS &
CELEBRATIONS

Grandma Enriqueta's Turnovers

Empanaditas de Mi Abuelita Enriqueta

*This is a recipe from my maternal grandmother.
My cousin Maguie rescued it and is very kindly sharing it so that
I can include it in this book. Thank you, Maguie!*

PREPARATION TIME: 20 minutes / **COOKING TIME:** 25 minutes
MAKES: approximately 20, depending on size

**500g plain flour, sifted ◆ 1 teaspoon baking powder
50g vegetable fat or pork lard ◆ Salt ◆ Warm water ◆ Vegetable oil for frying**

1 On a large, clean tabletop, mix the sifted flour, baking powder, vegetable fat or lard and salt. Add warm water, little by little, until you get a soft paste. Roll out the dough with a large rolling pin until it is very thin. Cut with a round cutter; the size depends on the size of empanada that you desire. Put your chosen filling inside, close and seal. Fry on both sides in very hot oil.

Suggested fillings:
Picadillo (see page 57)
Fish filling for Mexican Fish Pie (see page 76)
Basque-style Cod (see page 144)
Sautéed chorizo and potatoes, cheese, wild mushrooms and courgette flowers sautéed with onions and oregano

Sticky Almond and Pine Kernel Sweets
Bolitas de Faltriquera

I am not certain about the origin of this recipe, but it seems to be Spanish. My paternal grandmother used to make these delicious sweets, wrap them in colourful papers and serve them in little baskets. They contain ingredients that are expensive for Mexicans, such as almonds and pine kernels, so this is another opportunity for godparents to illustrate their wealth and forthcoming generosity towards their godchildren. These sweets can be served at the end of a breakfast. I don't know if it is a Mexican tradition to serve these at christenings, but it was certainly always a custom in my father's family.

PREPARATION TIME: 10 minutes, plus overnight cooling / COOKING TIME: 15–20 minutes
MAKES: about 90

400g canned condensed milk ◆ 4 egg yolks, beaten
125g ground almonds ◆ 85g ground pine kernels ◆ 125ml water
1 teaspoon vanilla essence ◆ 1 tablespoon dry sherry ◆ 225g caster or vanilla sugar

◆

1 Mix the condensed milk with the egg yolks. Add the ground almonds, pine kernels, water and vanilla. Put into a pan and simmer gently, stirring constantly until the paste forms a ball and you can see the base of the pan. This will take about 10 minutes.

2 Add the sherry and cook slowly for a further 5 minutes or until the mixture becomes a paste that is very thick and difficult to stir. It should stick together and you should easily see the base of the pan as you stir. Take off the heat and leave to cool, preferably overnight.

3 When it is cold and thick, pinch off a little of the paste and roll it in the palms of your hands. Make small balls the size of hazelnuts. Roll the balls in the caster or vanilla sugar. Place on a baking sheet and leave to chill in the refrigerator for about 1 hour.

4 Wrap the balls in individual pieces of colourful paper or in white paper for a christening.

Mexican Hot Chocolate
Chocolate a la Mexicana

Steamy cups of hot chocolate spiced with cinnamon are evocative of Mexico. Hot chocolate can be served with hot churros (fried batter snacks similar to doughnuts) in the evening or with pastries for breakfast. It is also served during the traditional breakfast that normally follows a christening or a first communion.

PREPARATION TIME: 5 minutes / **COOKING TIME:** 5 minutes / **MAKES:** 1 cup

2 teaspoons good-quality ground cocoa
1 teaspoon sugar, plus extra to taste ◆ ¼ teaspoon ground cinnamon
½ teaspoon ground almonds ◆ 250ml milk

◆

1 Make the chocolate mix by putting all the ingredients (except the milk) together in an empty, clean glass jar. Shake until completely combined.

2 Heat the milk in a pan and add the chocolate mix. Bring to the boil and reduce the heat. Simmer for about 2 minutes, stirring constantly. Use a small whisk to froth the milk. Serve hot.

Crêpes with Wild Mushrooms and Poblano Chilli Sauce

Crepas de Setas con Salsa de Chiles Poblanos

This is a delicious vegetarian dish that was served as breakfast at my first communion.

PREPARATION TIME: 40 minutes / **COOKING TIME:** 45 minutes / **SERVES:** 8

2 cups sifted flour ◆ 500ml milk ◆ 2 eggs
1 tablespoon vegetable oil ◆ 50g plus 1 tablespoon butter, melted
1 medium onion, finely chopped ◆ 2 cloves garlic, crushed ◆ 700g sliced, mixed
fresh wild mushrooms (e.g., porcini, shiitake and any others that you can find)
150g sliced courgette flowers ◆ 2 large poblano chillies, deseeded, grilled and peeled
(see page 133) ◆ 80ml milk ◆ 500ml soured cream ◆ Salt and pepper
170g grated cheddar cheese

◆

1 Preheat the oven to 240°C/475°F Gas Mark 9.

2 To make the crêpes, mix the flour, milk, egg and oil together in a bowl and leave to cool for 5 minutes to allow the batter to settle. Heat a medium-sized frying pan and brush with melted butter. When the frying pan starts to smoke, add enough batter to cover the base (half a ladleful is enough), tilting so that the batter spreads evenly. Fry until the edges are cooked, flip the crêpe and cook on the other side until golden in colour. Slide on to a large plate and reserve. Continue until all the batter is used.

3 To make the filling, melt 2 tablespoons of butter, add the onion and sauté until the onion is slightly translucent and soft. Add the garlic and cook for a further 1 minute. Add the wild mushrooms and courgette flowers and cook until soft.

4 To make the sauce, slice the chillies and put them in a blender with the milk and soured cream. Blend until puréed. Add salt and pepper to taste.

5 Put a crêpe in a baking dish and fill with some of the mushroom mixture. Fold in half and repeat with the rest of the crêpes. Cover with poblano sauce and sprinkle with the cheese.

6 Put in the preheated oven for 10 minutes, until the cheese is melted and golden. Serve.

Stuffed Poblanos in Walnut Sauce
Chiles en Nogada

This national dish is special because it can only be made in September, when tender walnuts are in season. It is ideal for weddings. If you happen to be in Mexico during September, try eating this at a good restaurant – it is truly memorable. Below is an adapted recipe from my mother's beloved godmother, Carmen.

PREPARATION TIME: 1 hour / **COOKING TIME:** 1 hour 30 minutes / **MAKES:** 12 chillies

12 medium-sized poblano chillies ◆ **1 medium onion, finely chopped** ◆ **2 cloves garlic, finely chopped** ◆ **300g fresh lean pork mince** ◆ **1 teaspoon ground cinnamon** ◆ **500ml pork or vegetable stock** ◆ **Pinch of sugar** ◆ **1 tablespoon flaked almonds** ◆ **1 tablespoon raisins** **1 tablespoon chopped green olives** ◆ **1 hard-boiled egg, chopped** ◆ **Salt and black pepper** **4 eggs, yolks and whites separated** ◆ **90g plain flour** ◆ **250g vegetable or corn oil** **100g shelled walnuts** ◆ **500ml single cream** ◆ **2 teaspoons breadcrumbs** **100g feta cheese** ◆ **125ml milk** ◆ **1 cup fresh pomegranate seeds**

1 Grill the chillies until blackened and put in a plastic bag. Wrap the bag and leave the chillies to steam for 5 minutes. Peel off the skins, make slits lengthways and remove the seeds and veins using rubber gloves.

2 To make the filling, sauté the onion and one clove of garlic. Add the meat, cinnamon, stock and sugar. Cook for 15 minutes, until the meat is cooked. Add the almonds, raisins, olives and hard-boiled egg. Season with salt and black pepper. Fill the chillies with the meat mixture.

3 In a separate bowl, beat the egg whites with an electric mixer until they form stiff peaks. Add two of the egg yolks and beat until incorporated.

4 Put the flour on a large plate and lightly coat the chillies. Dip them in the egg mixture. Heat the oil in a frying pan and fry the chillies until golden. Place on kitchen paper to absorb excess oil.

5 To make the sauce, mix the walnuts, cream, remaining garlic, breadcrumbs and feta cheese in a blender. If the sauce is too thick, add a little milk and blend.

6 Serve the poblanos on a large dish and pour the sauce over. Top with pomegranate seeds and serve at room temperature.

Wedding Biscuits
Galletas de Boda

Weddings in Mexico are great celebrations. In Mexico City, churches tend to cram weddings one after another on Friday and Saturday evenings, so you often see a bride, groom and guests waiting in line for the previous wedding to finish. In small villages, everybody is invited to the wedding and these biscuits are perfect to serve at the end of a meal to a large number of guests.

PREPARATION TIME: 30 minutes / **COOKING TIME:** 15 minutes / **MAKES:** 36

100g butter ◆ 250g caster sugar ◆ 100g plain flour
1 teaspoon vanilla essence ◆ 100g finely chopped hazelnuts
80g vanilla sugar

◆

1 Preheat the oven to 180°C/350°F/Gas Mark 4.

2 With an electric mixer, beat the butter and the caster sugar until creamy. Sift the flour and add to the butter and sugar mix. Add the vanilla extract and hazelnuts. Mix until well combined.

3 Divide the dough into small balls about 2cm in diameter and place on a greased baking sheet. Bake for 15 minutes or until cooked and golden.

4 Remove the baked biscuits from the oven and leave to cool completely on a wire rack. Roll each biscuit in the vanilla sugar.

5 Put the biscuits in small paper cases or arrange them in an attractive basket decorated with colourful paper.

Mama says...
To make vanilla sugar, add one vanilla pod to 450g sugar. Set aside for 3 weeks and then mix. Use to sweeten hot drinks as a sugar alternative.

Mole Sauce
Mole de Oaxaca

The Day of the Dead is a festival that is indigenous to Mexico and other Central American countries. It serves to remind us of departed souls on October 31st and the first two days of November. Although it's a colourful occasion, it's also quite solemn, as Mexicans believe the souls of their deceased loved ones will return to spend time with them. Mexicans usually make an altar or an ofrenda, where food offerings can be made to their dearly departed. Mole is a sauce that has become one of our national dishes and it is traditionally served to celebrate the return of the dead.

PREPARATION TIME: 1 hour / **COOKING TIME:** 1 hour 30 minutes / **SERVES:** 8

140g dried ancho chillies ◆ 85g pasilla chilli ◆ 85g mulato chilli ◆ 140g grilled, unpeeled tomatoes ◆ 250ml water ◆ 3 whole cloves ◆ 3 whole allspice berries
1 tablespoon fresh thyme leaves ◆ 1 tablespoon fresh marjoram leaves ◆ 1 tablespoon oregano ◆ 200g vegetable oil ◆ 50g sesame seeds ◆ 50g shelled, peeled peanuts
10 unpeeled almonds ◆ 50g raisins ◆ 1 small sliced onion
12 cloves garlic, peeled ◆ 1 large cinnamon stick, about 8cm long
1 ripe plantain, sliced ◆ 1 corn tortilla ◆ 2 tablespoons breadcrumbs
50g plain dark cooking chocolate ◆ Salt

1 Clean the chillies. Remove and reserve the seeds. Grill the chillies for 20 seconds on each side, rinse them in cold water and cover with boiling water. Soak for about 5 minutes.

2 In a heated frying pan, dry-fry the reserved chilli seeds and stir constantly, until blackened. (This process might make you cough, but it is part of the recipe – sorry!) Cover them with cold water and leave for 5 minutes. Remove the seeds from the frying pan and rinse. Put in the blender.

3 Add the grilled tomatoes. Add the water, cloves, allspice, thyme, marjoram and oregano.

4 Heat the oil in a small frying pan and fry the sesame seeds until golden brown (a few seconds). Drain the sesame seeds, returning the drained oil

to the frying pan afterwards. Add the sesame seeds to the blender and mix well with other ingredients.

5 Fry the peanuts, almonds, raisins, onion, garlic, cinnamon and plantain in oil for 5 minutes. Drain them and put in the blender. Add the tortilla and bread crumbs. Blend gradually, adding water to aid the blending process.

6 Heat some oil in another pan. Add the blended ingredients and fry, stirring occasionally, for about 15 minutes. Meanwhile, add the chillies to the blender with 475ml of the soaking water. Grind them until soft. Once blended, add them to the fried ingredients in the pan. Add the chocolate and cook for a further 5 minutes. Add about 1 litre of stock and continue cooking for a further 35 minutes. Add salt to taste.

7 If you are making tamales, you can use some of the fat skimmed from the top of the sauce and add it to the dough. This will give a nice colour as well as a hint of mole flavour.

8 Serve the sauce with poached chicken or turkey pieces. Garnish with roasted sesame seeds, crumbled feta cheese, raw onions and soured cream.

Bread of the Dead
Pan de Muerto

This recipe produces a bread that is more rustic than the one that is so often produced in Mexico these days. It takes time to make, but your patience will be rewarded with a delicious bread that tastes the way it did in the old days.

PREPARATION TIME: 40 minutes, plus 24 hours resting time / **COOKING TIME:** 1 hour / **SERVES:** 6–8

180ml tepid water ◆ 2 tablespoons dried yeast ◆ 380g plain flour
225g caster sugar ◆ 1 teaspoon salt ◆ 3 large eggs ◆ 250ml vegetable oil
1 tablespoon finely grated orange rind ◆ 1 teaspoon vanilla essence ◆ Milk to glaze
4 tablespoons sugar

◆

1 In a small bowl, mix the water and yeast. Make sure the yeast disperses completely.

2 Put the flour in the large bowl of an electric mixer. Add the water and yeast mixture and stir a little. Add the sugar, salt, eggs, oil, orange rind and vanilla essence.

3 Mix using the flat paddle of the mixer at a medium speed for about 10 minutes. The dough is ready when it looks translucent against the light when stretched by hand. Place the dough in a deep bowl and cover with cling film. Leave to cool in a warm place, away from draughts, for 24 hours, until doubled in volume.

4 Preheat the oven to 180°C/350°F/Gas Mark 4.

5 Remove the dough from the bowl and place on a clean, lightly floured surface. Do not add extra flour to the dough. Cut the dough in half and remove one-third of each half with your hands. Reserve these thirds. Roll the remaining two-thirds of each half into two balls and place on an oiled baking sheet. Shape the two reserved thirds of the dough into large ropes. Cut them in half and place on top of each ball of bread, in the shape of a cross. If you want to be very authentic, you can shape these ropes like bones, a little fatter at the ends and thinner in the middle. Brush the dough with milk and sprinkle on the sugar.

6 Bake for 20 minutes in the preheated oven, then reduce the heat to 150°C/300°F/Gas Mark 2 for 20 minutes. Reduce the temperature to

120°C/250°F/Gas Mark ½ and bake for a further 20 minutes. When fully baked, the bread should sound hollow when tapped on the base.

7 Remove from the oven and leave to cool on a wire rack before serving.

Mexican-style Coffee
Café de Olla

This is the traditional way to drink coffee in Mexico. It is usually sweetened with brown sugar and spiced with cinnamon. It is often served at events that take place in the evening, when it can be cold, such as during the vigil on the Day of the Dead or during a posada party. Some people pour in a little rum or firewater to help keep the heat in the body!

PREPARATION TIME: 5 minutes / **COOKING TIME:** 5 minutes / **SERVES:** 4

**1 litre water ◆ 2 tablespoons freshly ground coffee (or more, if you like strong coffee)
1 stick cinnamon ◆ 2 tablespoons dark brown sugar ◆ 5 whole cloves
Rind of ¼ orange**

◆

1 Heat the water and add all the coffee, cinnamon, sugar, cloves and rind. Bring to the boil and remove from the heat. Leave to rest for about 2 minutes so the flavours can develop. Taste and add more sugar if required (it should taste fairly sweet).

2 Pour through a fine sieve into an attractive coffeepot. Serve in clay cups. Do not add cream or milk.

Sugar Skulls
Calaveritas de Azúcar

Sugar skulls are traditionally given to children during the celebrations of the Day of the Dead. They are also put at the altar as an offering to the dead. Some make their skulls with chocolate or amaranth seeds. There are entire towns whose main craft during this time is the making of these skulls. Here is a simple recipe for making them with icing sugar.

PREPARATION TIME: 20 minutes / **DRYING TIME:** overnight / **SERVES:** approximately 5

1kg icing sugar ◆ Juice of 1 lime ◆ 400g canned condensed milk
Coloured icing pens, to decorate (or make your own by dissolving 1–2 drops
food colouring in a little water mixed with icing sugar)

1 Put the sugar in a bowl and add the lime juice and condensed milk gradually. Be careful not to add too much liquid too quickly. Mix by hand until a paste is formed that can be easily moulded and does not stick to the hands. Add more sugar if necessary.

2 Divide the paste into five equal-sized pieces and mould each into a skull shape. Use a cocktail stick to make holes to resemble the eyes and teeth. Leave to dry.

3 Decorate each skull with coloured icing, using a piping bag. Add sequins as eyes and write the names of friends with icing on the skulls' foreheads. Give as gifts to friends to celebrate the Day of the Dead.

Pumpkin Pudding

Calabaza en Tacha

This dessert is traditionally served during the celebrations of the Day of the Dead. These celebrations coincide with the pumpkin harvest, so here is a special recipe to celebrate the return of our departed to earth and an offering of the year's bounty.

PREPARATION TIME: 15 minutes / **COOKING TIME:** 25 minutes / **SERVES:** 8–10

3.2kg pumpkin ◆ 500ml water
1kg black treacle ◆ 2 sticks cinnamon ◆ 5 cloves

◆

1 Using a sharp knife, cut the pumpkin flesh into large pieces, leaving the seeds. Do not peel. Be careful when cutting pumpkin, as the skin can be tough and the knife can easily slip.

2 In a large saucepan, heat the water and add the pumpkin, treacle, cinnamon and cloves.

Cover and cook the pumpkin over a low heat, until soft and slightly mushy. Stir occasionally so the pumpkin does not stick to the pan.

3 If you like, toast some sesame seeds and sprinkle over the pumpkin before serving, or drizzle with a little warm milk or single cream.

Oyster Soup

Sopa de Ostiones

The Christmas period is a time when Mexicans, like many other people in the world, like to feed their families with the best food they can buy. On Christmas Eve, my Uncle Fernando would make oyster soup – his speciality – as a starter. Unfortunately, I don't have Uncle Fernando's exact recipe for oyster soup, but I found another recipe written by an uncle of his. It was in a fabulous book that was handwritten in 1932 and is a real legacy from my mother.

PREPARATION TIME: 20 minutes / COOKING TIME: 40 minutes / SERVES: 6–8

80ml butter, softened ◆ 3 tablespoons plain flour ◆ 1 litre warm milk
80ml single cream ◆ Salt ◆ Pinch of white pepper ◆ Pinch of nutmeg
4 leeks, finely sliced ◆ 2 tablespoons fresh flat-leaf parsley, finely chopped
750g fresh oysters, shucked and cleaned ◆ 500g croûtons

1 In a large pan, heat the butter, add the flour and stir together without burning the mixture.

2 Add the milk, cream, salt, white pepper, nutmeg, leeks and parsley. When the mixture starts to boil, add the oysters. Simmer gently for 25 minutes.

3 Serve hot in individual serving bowls and sprinkle with croûtons.

Mama says...
Try substituting scallops or crabmeat for the oysters, or why not try a mixture of all three?

Basque-style Cod
Bacalao a la Viscaina

Dried cod is a real luxury in Mexico; it arrives in November on Spanish and Norwegian boats. I remember travelling with my father to the centre of the city to find an old-fashioned Spanish deli that sold this cod. My family arrived in Mexico in the 1820s from the Basque province of Vizcaya, and this recipe comes from that very province – it is my maternal grandmother's recipe. This dish is very rich. My father really enjoys making it, especially on Christmas Eve, when he serves it up as a second course after my Uncle Fernando's Oyster Soup (see page 143). He takes so much care with it that it can take him a whole day to prepare. Mind you, all that preparation results in a most delicious dish.

PREPARATION TIME: 2 hours, plus overnight soaking / COOKING TIME: 4–5 hours / SERVES: 14–16

**1kg dried salt cod ◆ 1 litre good-quality Spanish olive oil
4 large onions, finely chopped ◆ 10 cloves garlic, finely chopped
1 large bunch fresh flat-leaf parsley, finely chopped ◆ 2kg ripe tomatoes, finely chopped**

◆

1 Soak the dried salt cod in a bowl of water and leave for 2 hours. Rinse and soak again for 3 hours more. Rinse once more and soak overnight.

2 Fill a pan with salted water and cook the cod for 1 hour. Remove from the heat, leave to cool and shred lightly with your fingers. Remove any fins, skin or bones and discard. Reserve the fish.

3 In another large pan, heat half the oil and sauté the onion gently, until transparent and soft.

Add the garlic and continue frying until soft (add more oil if necessary). Add the parsley and continue frying until the parsley darkens in colour and the edges fold inwards. Add the tomatoes and cook for about 45 minutes, stirring often until the sauce no longer tastes acidic. At this point, add a little more oil. Whenever the sauce looks dry during cooking, add more oil.

4 When the sauce is ready, add the cod. Cook for 30 minutes to allow the flavours to develop.

5 Serve hot, as a course during your Christmas meal or use as a filling for empanadas. The day after Christmas, serve any leftover fish in a bridge roll. The flavours will have developed overnight and fresh bread complements the fish perfectly.

Christmas Punch
Ponche Navideño

This warming punch contains winter fruits that grow in Mexico. Some of these are not available in the UK, so I have found substitutes. This punch is a good alternative to mulled wine. (Not that mulled wine needs an alternative – I'd say try both! It's Christmas time!)

PREPARATION TIME: 15 minutes / **COOKING TIME:** 1 hour / **SERVES:** 24

600g black treacle ◆ 3½ litres water ◆ 250g dried apricots, halved (as a substitute for tejocotes) ◆ 250g guavas, quartered ◆ 250g stoned prunes, halved 250g sugar cane, cut into 2.5cm pieces ◆ 250ml rum or whisky

1 Dissolve the treacle in the water and add the fruit and sugar cane. Heat and simmer gently until the fruit is cooked through, about 1 hour.

2 Add the rum or whisky, and a little more sugar if you prefer a sweeter taste. Serve hot in a large serving bowl. Spoon into individual cups with a ladle.

Epiphany Bread
Rosca de Reyes

Once New Year celebrations are over, Epiphany arrives – the evening when the three wise men arrived bearing gifts to greet baby Jesus. In parts of Mexico and Spain, this date is considered very important, and it is actually the three wise men (or kings, as they are known in Mexico) who bring gifts to the children, instead of Santa Claus. January 5th is marked with a special evening celebration, where families get together and eat a rosca, a lavishly decorated, ring-shaped cake. Inside the cake is hidden a little token (usually a small plastic baby). Whoever receives the token must invite everyone to a party on February 2nd, the day of the Candelaria – the date of purification to celebrate the approach of spring and the advent of Lent.

PREPARATION TIME: 40 minutes, plus 24 hours resting / **COOKING TIME:** 1 hour / **SERVES:** 6–8

180ml tepid water ◆ 2 tablespoons dried yeast
380g plain flour ◆ 225g caster sugar ◆ 1 teaspoon salt
3 large eggs ◆ 250ml vegetable oil ◆ 1 tablespoon finely grated orange rind
1 teaspoon vanilla essence ◆ Milk to glaze ◆ Sugar to decorate ◆ 50g chopped, candied angelica ◆ 100g dried fruits (a mix of sliced apricots and prunes) ◆ 2 tablespoons halved glacé cherries ◆ 50g sliced dates

1 In a small bowl, mix the water and yeast. Make sure the yeast disperses well and is completely incorporated. Put the flour in the bowl of an electric mixer. Add the water and yeast mixture and mix for about 1 minute.

2 Add the sugar, salt, eggs, oil, rind and vanilla. Mix using the flat spatula of the mixer at a medium speed for about 10 minutes. The dough is ready when it looks translucent against the light when

stretched by hand. Place the dough in a deep bowl and cover with cling film. Place the dough in a warm, draught-free place for 24 hours, until doubled in volume.

3 Preheat the oven to 180°C/350°F/Gas Mark 4. Remove the dough from the bowl and place on a clean and lightly floured surface. Divide the dough in half.

4 Shape one half into a large sausage shape and then curl around into a ring. Repeat with the other half of dough. If the dough is too sticky to handle, add some flour to your hands and to the work surface. Do not add flour directly to the dough. Put a little metal token inside the centre of each ring (some people use a clean coin). Place the rings on an oiled baking sheet.

5 Brush each ring of dough with milk and sprinkle on some sugar. Decorate with the angelica, dried fruits, cherries and dates.

6 Bake in the preheated oven for 20 minutes, then reduce the temperature to 150°C/300°F/Gas Mark 2 for a further 20 minutes. Reduce to 120°C/250°F/Gas Mark ½ and bake for a further 20 minutes.

7 When cooked, the base of the bread should sound hollow when tapped with your fingers. Remove from the oven and leave to cool on a wire rack.

Mama says...
Warn your friends that there is a little metal token in the bread. Otherwise, they might break a tooth when taking a bite! If you want to use a plastic baby as a token, insert it from underneath after the loaves have baked and cooled.

Uncle Javier's Coconut Dessert
Cocada

This recipe comes from a fantastic recipe book that my uncle wrote (in his beautiful handwriting) back in 1932. My father, who has a great sweet tooth, found this recipe many years ago and has made it ever since. The recipe calls for freshly shredded coconut, but because fresh coconut can be tricky to peel and shred, I have adapted this recipe using dried coconut, which works very well. It's perfect for serving at outdoor summer celebrations.

PREPARATION TIME: 10 minutes / **COOKING TIME:** 35 minutes / **SERVES:** 8–10

750g brown sugar ◆ 1 litre milk
500g desiccated coconut ◆ 4 egg yolks

1 Put the brown sugar in a heavy-based saucepan and add a little water. Heat, stirring constantly. Add almost all the milk and the coconut. Bring to just below boiling point and keep stirring.

2 Beat the egg yolks with the remaining milk and add to the pan. Continue stirring for about 15 minutes. The mixture will become creamy, thick and frothy. The coconut will also change texture.

3 Remove from the heat and leave to cool slightly. Transfer to a serving dish and serve at room temperature. Store in the refrigerator for up to 1 week.

Mama says...
Add a little sherry or rum and raisins towards the end of the cooking time. Pour the dessert into a heatproof dish and grill the surface, until it turns a golden brown colour, before serving.

Coffee Flan

Flan de Café

All Mexican families have their own recipe for flan. It is a very traditional dessert with Spanish roots and is often served at parties. This is my mother's recipe. I have made this again and again over the years for friends and family. I have also used the recipe as part of my catering repertoire and have taught it to many people who love it!

PREPARATION TIME: 10 minutes / **COOKING TIME:** 1 hour 15 minutes / **SERVES:** 6

300g brown sugar ◆ 2 eggs plus 2 egg yolks
290ml single cream ◆ 400g canned condensed milk
15ml strong coffee or 2 teaspoons instant coffee

1 Caramelize the sugar in a heavy-based saucepan, stirring constantly with a wooden spoon until fairly dark in colour (the darker it is, the stronger-tasting the caramel). Be careful not to burn yourself with the hot, bubbling sugar.

2 Carefully pour the caramel into a medium-sized heatproof dish or bowl and turn slowly so that the bowl is coated with the caramel.

3 Preheat the oven to 180°C/350°F/Gas Mark 4. Beat the eggs and egg yolks in another bowl until creamy. Add the cream, condensed milk and coffee. Mix well, ensuring the coffee powder has completely dissolved.

4 Pour this mixture into the caramel-coated dish and cook in a bain-marie in the preheated oven for 1 hour 15 minutes or until a knife inserted into the centre comes out clean.

5 Remove the dish from the bain-marie and leave to cool. Remove the caramel custard from the dish and serve.

Mama says...
For the bain-marie, use a deep rectangular tin and put the dish of caramel inside. Pour enough water into the tin to come halfway up the side of the dish. Bake and add more water if the tin looks dry.

Aunt Margarita's Courgette Cake
Pastel de Calabacitas de la Tía Margarita

Aunt Margarita is my mother's sister and her speciality is baking. Here is one of her many recipes. Try baking this cake for a birthday party – it makes an unusual change from traditional celebration cakes. Courgette sounds like a weird ingredient for a cake, but it works very well, just like beetroot – but that's another story!

PREPARATION TIME: 30 minutes / **COOKING TIME:** 40 minutes / **SERVES:** 10

180g plain flour ◆ 1 teaspoon baking powder ◆ 1 tablespoon ground cinnamon
340g caster sugar ◆ 3 large eggs ◆ 250ml vegetable oil
1 teaspoon salt ◆ 345g grated courgette ◆ 1 tablespoon chopped walnuts
110g butter, for greasing

1 Preheat the oven to 180°C/350°F/Gas Mark 4.

2 Sift the flour and baking powder together into a bowl.

3 Mix the cinnamon and sugar together in another bowl.

4 In another large bowl, beat the eggs with a whisk until they look fluffy. Add the sugar and cinnamon mixture to the eggs. Add the oil and salt and continue beating. Add the courgettes, walnuts and the sifted flour and baking powder. Stir well to mix.

5 Brush a 28 x 18 x 5-cm tin with melted butter before lining with baking paper. Spoon the mixture into the tin.

6 Bake the cake in the centre of the preheated oven for about 40 minutes or until firm. Check to see if the cake is ready by sticking a skewer in the centre. If it comes out clean, the cake is ready.

7 Remove from the oven and leave to cool for about 5 minutes. Remove from the tin and leave to cool completely on a wire rack before serving.

Traditional Mexican Drink
Atole

Atole is a pre-Hispanic drink that consists of corn and water. It is widely drunk in Mexico, especially at christenings and first communions. When it is made with cocoa, it is called champurrado, which is also served at these events.

PREPARATION TIME: 10 minutes / COOKING TIME: 10 minutes / SERVES: 4

85g masa harina ◆ 250ml milk ◆ 750ml water
110g brown sugar ◆ 1 stick cinnamon
1 teaspoon vanilla essence ◆ 1 teaspoon cornflour

1 Combine all the ingredients in a large saucepan and heat. Bring to the boil and leave to simmer gently for 10 minutes, stirring occasionally. Pass through a fine sieve and return to the heat for a further 5 minutes to thicken. If it is too runny, add more cornflour dissolved in a little cold water.

Mama says...
You can add puréed fruit to the original mixture and then strain. Some people also add strawberries or pineapple.

Maguie's Lime Ice Cream
Helado de Limón de Maguie

This is another one of my cousin Maguie's favourite party recipes, loved by adults and children alike. It is not a sorbet, but an ice cream made with Mexican limes – quite unusual. When buying limes, try to find small fruit with thin skins, as these are the juiciest.

PREPARATION TIME: 35 minutes / **FREEZING TIME:** 4–5 hours / **SERVES:** 4

**340g canned evaporated milk ◆ 1¼ cups sugar
Juice of 3 limes ◆ 2 large eggs, separated ◆ 5 drops natural green food colouring**

1 Put the milk in a large bowl and place in the freezer for 1 hour or more, until ice crystals form on the surface.

2 Remove the milk from the freezer and beat with a hand-held blender until it doubles in size. Add half the sugar and the lime juice and mix together.

3 In another bowl, beat the egg yolks with half of the remaining sugar until pale in colour. In a separate bowl, beat the egg whites with the remaining sugar until stiff peaks form. With a metal spoon, add the milk, sugar, lime mixture and the beaten egg yolks together. Fold in the egg white carefully. Add the green food colouring and gently mix together.

4 Transfer the mixture to a shallow dish and place in the freezer for 4–5 hours, until set. Serve in individual glass cups decorated with a slice of lime.

Glossary

Adobo: A vinegar-based seasoning or marinade.

Ancho chilli: Dried red poblano chilli with a mild, fruity flavour.

Atole: A traditional Mexican drink made by combining masa harina with milk, sugar, spices and water. Fruit is sometimes added. When cocoa powder is added, the drink is called *champurrado*.

Bain-marie: A large tin of hot water in which a smaller pan is placed for gentle cooking. The term may also be applied to a double pan with water in the base.

Basmati rice: A high-quality rice from India.

Bisquet: A Mexican biscuit that is similar to a scone, made with yeast and served buttered or with jam as a snack with coffee.

Cactus: The paddles of the prickly pear cactus (nopales or nopalitos) are used as a vegetable in Mexican cuisine. They are available canned.

Candelaria: The feast of Candlemas, held on 2 February to celebrate the purification of the Virgin Mary and the presentation of Christ in the Temple.

Champurrado: Chocolate-flavoured atole.

Chilaquiles: Chilaquiles is a dish of tortilla strips baked with tomatillos or tomato sauce and serrano chillies.

Chipotle chilli: A smoke-dried, hot red jalapeño chilli.

Chorizo: A Spanish sausage made of cured pork, mildly spiced and flavoured with paprika and garlic.

Crêpe: A thin pancake.

Day of the Dead: A feast common in Mexico and other countries of Central America, celebrated from 31 October to 2 November. Apart from dishes enjoyed by the living, food offerings may be made to the dead, who are believed to return at this time of year.

Enchilada: Enchiladas are made by rolling a tortilla around a filling to make a tube. The filled tortillas are placed in a dish, covered with sauce and baked or grilled.

Epiphany: The Epiphany is the feast celebrating the arrival of the Magi bearing gifts for the infant Jesus. Children in parts of Spain and Mexico receive presents on 5 January rather than on Christmas Day.

Grenadine: A cordial syrup made from pomegranate juice.

Guacamole: A sauce made of mashed avocado, usually served as a dip with tortilla chips. Other ingredients may include serrano chillies, garlic and diced tomatoes.

Guajillo chilli: Dried chillies slightly hotter than ancho or mulato chillies, with an acidic taste.

Habañero chilli: Also known as a 'Scotch bonnet chilli', it is a very hot red chilli pepper that can be used fresh or dried.

Jalapeño chilli: Medium-hot, plump green or red chilli pepper. Jalapeños are popular as a pickle in Mexico. Smoke-dried jalapeños are called chipotle chillies.

Masa harina: Cornmeal or corn flour made by cooking dried white corn in lime water and grinding to a paste. Masa harina is also known as 'tortilla flour'.

Molcajete: The Mexican mortar, traditionally made of volcanic rock. The pestle, also made of volcanic rock, is called a *tejolote*. The molcajete and tejolote are used for grinding chillies, garlic, herbs and spices and also for making fresh salsas and guacamole.

Mole: A slow-cooked stew of meat or poultry.

Mulato chilli: Dried chilli with a mild, smoky taste.

Olive oil, extra virgin: Oil produced by the first cold pressing of the olives.

Pasilla chilli: Long, dark, slender chilli of medium heat and rich flavour.

Pesto: In Italian cuisine, a dressing based on olive oil, basil and pine kernels. A version suitable for Mexican cuisine can be made by caramelising onions with coriander in butter.

Picadillo: Made from ground meat, spices, almonds, raisins and tomatoes. It can be used as a filling in many different recipes.

Pimenton: A powder made from ground dried peppers. Pimenton dulce can be used to thicken sauces, but pimenton picante, which is used as a seasoning, is too hot for this purpose.

Piquillo: A red pepper sold preserved in oil or brine.

Poblano chilli: A large, mild to medium-hot, green or red chilli pepper. Dried poblano chillies are known as 'ancho chillies'.

Porcini: Large edible mushrooms; also known as 'ceps'. They are available dried.

Salpicón: Salpicón is a salad based on beef, which is braised and then marinated and served on a bed of lettuce with cold mixed vegetables and potatoes.

Salsa: A sauce, dressing or dip made by combining fresh vegetables and seasonings and usually served as a side dish with meat or fish. Salsas can be cooked or uncooked.

Serrano chilli: Also known as 'bird's-eye chillies', serranos are slender, thin-skinned chillies, frequently used while still green. Both the red and green peppers are used in cooked dishes and can be pickled.

Shiitake: A dark mushroom also known as an 'oyster mushroom'; they are now widely available in supermarkets.

Soffritto: Carrots, celery, onions, garlic and herbs fried in olive oil and used as a base for sauces, soups and casseroles in Italian cuisine. A Mexican version can be made with tomatoes, onions, garlic, chipotles and corn oil.

Taco: Made of tortilla, stuffed with a filling and then rolled. They can be soft or crispy and are traditionally eaten with salsa or guacamole.

Tamale: A dumpling made of cornmeal, wrapped in banana leaves or corn husks and steamed. They are usually stuffed with a sweet or savoury filling.

Tempura: A Japanese dish in which pieces of meat, fish or vegetables are dipped in batter and fried.

Tequila: A twice-distilled spirit made from the sap of the blue agave plant. The first distillation makes mescal. Tequila production is subject to strictly regulated quality control.

Tomatillo: Also known as a 'Mexican green tomato', a tomatillo is actually a fruit of the physalis plant. Fresh tomatillos resemble tomatoes but have a papery husk. They are available canned.

Tortilla: A thin bread made from corn or wheat flour and used as the basis for many Mexican dishes.

Tostada: An individual corn tortilla fried and served with toppings.

Index

Acknowledgements

To my mother, for being the most wonderful mother anyone could have; thank you for being wise, understanding and unobtrusive. Thank you for teaching me to cook and to not be fearful of life. Thank you for keeping all those books and recipes and photos as well; you were right, it is not clutter after all.

To my father, for taking me to all kinds of eateries since my early childhood, for bringing to my life the love of food that he has and for being so enthusiastic about food and eating. Thank you for being my eating accomplice and for the fun and laughter too!

To Oliver, my pillar of strength, for being a wonderful and understanding husband who has supported me with all of my mad projects. Thank you for your pep talks, patience and for being so loving through the years.

To Maguie and Raul, my dear cousins, who brought my mother over at the time of writing this book, for digging into family archives and for providing me with recipes and photos. Maguie, thank you for being my English teacher when I was eight, as well.

To my relatives, both in Mexico and the UK, thank you for your food and support, especially to cousin Mimi, for being my lovely big "sister" and to Auntie Irma, for all the lunches throughout my childhood and the fun times at Tepotzotlan.

To Paz and Jean Smith, thank you for your friendship, support and recipes – all my love forever.

To the School of Humanities at Birkbeck College, thank you for being patient and allowing me extra time to finish my course work in order to finish this book in time.

To Camilla and all at Divertimenti, for their continuous support, flexibility and inspiration.

To Rosie, Eric and all the staff at Books for Cooks, thank you for believing in me and giving me my first opportunity to teach.

To my testers and supportive friends: Nicky, Jane, Frederique, Lucy and Mark, Lorena, Sue and Ken, Michael, Shauna, Robin, Ruth, Nick, and Carolina and all the others that tested and offered to test recipes.

To Celia Brooks-Brown and Ursula Ferrigno, thanks for the words of encouragement.

My sincere thanks go to all the people that I have met on this journey, people who have encouraged me to continue, thank you for your support and for believing in me.

I have tried to think of all the relevant people here but I am sure that some are missing; it is not that you are not important or that I am not grateful, but there is only a certain amount of space here. You know I am grateful to you. Thank you.

Picture Credits

Mama says... When deseeding chillies, be as careful as possible. Try to wear rubber gloves and avoid rubbing your eyes.